Skills for

BRITISH ECONOMIC AND SOCIAL HISTORY

GCSE History Companions

Other history titles by Philip Sauvain:

Hulton New Histories:
  1 Tribes and Tribunes
  2 Serf and Crusader
  3 Crown and Parliament
  4 Forge and Factory
  5 War and Peace
  Teacher's Book

British Economic and Social History – Book 1 1700–1870
                              Book 2 1850–present day

GCSE History Companions:
  Skills for Modern World History
  Skills for British and European History

Modern World History – 1919 onwards

European and World History – 1815–1919

Lively History:
  Town and Country – 1485–1789
  Empire, City and Industry – 1789–1901
  Conflict, Science and Society: The Twentieth Century

Further history titles from Stanley Thornes and Hulton include:

Kelly: *A World of Change: Britain in the Early Modern Age 1450–1700*
  World of Change Topic Books:
    A City at War: Oxford 1642–46
    Elizabeth & Akbar: Portraits of Power
    Scolding Tongues: The Persecution of 'Witches'
    Bare Ruined Choirs: The Fate of a Welsh Abbey
    Exploring Other Civilisations
    Children in Tudor England
    The Cromwell Family
    To the New World: The Founding of Pennsylvania

Leeds: *Peace and War: A First Source Book*

Whiting (series co-ordinator): *Footprints:*
  Industry
  The Countryside
  Towns
  Churches

Archer & Shepley: *Witnessing History* (Oral history for GCSE)

Whiting: *Crime and Punishment: A Study Across Time*
        (Study book and Teacher's Resource book)

Simpson: *Changing Horizons: Britain 1914–1980*

Simpson: *Working with Sources: Case Studies in Twentieth Century History*

Skills for

BRITISH ECONOMIC AND SOCIAL HISTORY

GCSE History Companions

PHILIP SAUVAIN

STANLEY THORNES (PUBLISHERS) LTD

First published in 1988 by:
Stanley Thornes (Publishers) Ltd
Old Station Drive
Leckhampton
CHELTENHAM GL53 0DN
England

Reprinted 1989

British Library Cataloguing in Publication Data

Sauvain, Philip, *1933–*
    Skills for British economic and social
    history—(GCSE history companion)
    1. England. Secondary schools. Curriculum
    subjects. History study techniques
    I. Title   II. Series
    907′.1242

    ISBN 0–85950–825–0

Cover illustration: *The Dinner Hour, Wigan* by Eyre Crowe, reproduced by kind permission of Manchester City Art Galleries.

Typeset by Tech-Set, Gateshead, Tyne & Wear
in 10½/12½ Times
Printed and bound in Great Britain at The Bath Press, Avon

Contents

Acknowledgements vi

Introduction 1
Our Links with the Past 1

Testing Historical Evidence 4
What is Historical Evidence? 4
Has the Evidence been Altered? 16
Fact or Opinion? 19
Accuracy and Reliability 23
Bias and Prejudice 27
Gaps and Contradictions 35
Eyewitnesses and Hearsay Evidence 40

Different Types of Historical Evidence 47
Relics from the Past 47
Documentary Evidence 52
Newspapers and Magazines 57
Journals, Diaries and Letters 59
Memoirs and Oral History 64
Using Propaganda and Adverts 65

Evidence from Fiction 71
Evidence on Maps 74
Facts from Pictures 78
Facts from Photographs 92
Evidence in Sound and on Film 97
Facts from Statistics 100

Working as a Historian 104
Similarities and Differences 104
How Things Change 108
Imagining the Past 114
Cause and Consequence 117
Selecting Relevant Information 122
For and Against 123
Reaching a Conclusion 126

Summary Checklists 129

Index 135
Concepts, Skills and Sources 135
Themes in Economic and Social History 135

Acknowledgements

The author and publishers are grateful to the following for supplying and giving permission to reproduce prints and artwork:

BBC Hulton Picture Library, pages 34, 58, 78, 96 (below), 111, 120, 128; City of Manchester Art Galleries, page 90; Essex County Record Office, page 92; Guildhall Library, pages 114, 121; ICI, page 23; Illustrated London News, pages 21, 80; Manchester Public Libraries, page 46; Mary Evans Picture Library for illustration from *The English Illustrated Magazine*, page 42; National Portrait Gallery, page 18; *Punch*, page 86; Sport and General Press Agency, page 97; Topham Picture Library, page 8; TUC, page 37 (left); University of Reading, Institute of Agricultural History and Museum of English Rural Life, page 12.

The author and publishers are also grateful to the following for permission to reproduce text extracts:

Daily Mail for extracts from the *Daily Chronicle* and *Daily Mail*, page 58; Mail Newspapers plc, page 55; Mirror Group Newspapers, page 56; News International, page 56; *The Guardian*, page 56; TUC for extract from the *British Worker*, page 58.

Introduction

OUR LINKS WITH THE PAST

In 1983 the *Sunday Times* carried a report in which a journalist wrote:

> Last Tuesday I shook hands with a man who, when he was two,
> shook hands with a soldier who fought at the battle of Waterloo.
> For a moment I touched history.

Links with the past like this can be experienced every day. Your great grandmother knew people who lived at the time of the Crimean War, from 1854 to 1856. She might have had a great grandmother herself who travelled in a stage coach in the 1820s, or cheered when news of Nelson's victory at Trafalgar reached her town in 1805!

You can see and touch the past in the buildings and monuments near your home. Churches, castles, abbeys, mansions, houses, mills, paintings and photographs show us what buildings and people looked like in the past. Documents, books and newspapers also tell us what happened in the past. We call this *historical evidence*.

Workhouse in Stowmarket – a link with the Poor Law

We need to know about the past in order to understand the present. Only if we find out about the early history of education, for example, can we understand why the churches still play an important part in the running of Britain's schools. Only if we know what happened during the Industrial Revolution can we explain why great towns and cities grew up in the North and why they declined.

With every topic you study in social and economic history you will find a local link with the past. Blocked-up windows in an old building may remind you that many people bricked up their windows rather than pay the window tax in the years before 1851 (when it was repealed). The workhouse, often used nowadays as a home for old people, recalls the harsh conditions in which the poor and needy lived before the coming of the Welfare State in the twentieth century.

Checklist — **The Link with the Past**

Go through this checklist when you start a new topic in social and economic history.

1   *Find out if there are any features, such as buildings, monuments, street names, or house names near your home which link up in some way with the topic.*

2   *Which of your living relatives (if any) were alive for part of the time covered by the topic? What do they remember about this period?*

3   *What things from the past can you find in your local museum or library which link up with this topic?*

Going through the Checklist

Suppose you are studying the topic of 'Health and Medicine since 1700'. This is how you might go through the checklist.

1   *Find out if there are any features, such as buildings, monuments, street names, or house names near your home which link up in some way with the topic.*

You may discover that a local hospital was first built as an infirmary in the Victorian period. There may be a monument in a local church to the victims of a cholera or typhoid epidemic in the nineteenth century. In a large city you may discover that some of the streets are named after leading figures in health and medicine, such as Nightingale Terrace or Pasteur Street. Some streets may be named after local people who gave money to build a hospital.

2   *Which of your living relatives (if any) were alive for part of the time covered by the topic? What do they remember about this period?*

Your grandparents may be able to tell you about diseases which were much more common fifty years ago than they are today, such as diphtheria, whooping cough, and poliomyelitis. Ask them if their tonsils were removed, and how it was done.

3   *What things from the past can you find in your local museum or library which link up with this topic?*

Look at the advertisements in a Victorian magazine in the library or at old medicine bottles in a museum. Some medicines promised to cure or relieve most known illnesses!

EXERCISES AND ACTIVITIES

1   *Find out the dates of birth and death of your ancestors. Compile a family tree. It may show you that people had much bigger families eighty years ago than they do today. Many more babies died then than today.*

2   *Find out which of the museums near your home has exhibits which will help you discover more about the social and economic history of the period you are studying.*

Testing Historical Evidence

WHAT IS HISTORICAL EVIDENCE?

Historians can use only a few of the many facts of economic and social history. This is why they have to select those facts they think are most important, such as the invention of the spinning jenny by James Hargreaves in 1767 and the invention of the spinning mule by Samuel Crompton in 1779. These are *crucial* facts because they helped to change the history of the textile industry.

In addition, historians also select a few of the many facts which tell us something about the everyday life of ordinary people at the time when important changes were being made. Facts like these might include a report about the injuries suffered by a young girl working in a cotton mill in the 1830s, or a description of a day in a woollen mill in the 1880s. They help us to imagine what life was really like in the past, and show the sacrifices that ordinary people had to make in the name of progress. Yet these are *not* crucial facts. Similar examples, chosen from cases recorded in other textile mills, would serve just as well to illustrate the problems created by the Industrial Revolution.

Facts are only facts if they can be proved. We need evidence that they are facts and not something which a writer has made up. This means that we need to know the *source* or authority for each fact. Historians divide these historical sources into two main types.

Primary sources always date back to the actual time in the past when an event occurred. They are primary sources because they are based on what people saw, or heard, or created at the time. These primary sources may be in the form of words – such as a book, document, or letter. They may be in the shape of a building, an article of clothing, or some other relic you can touch. Some of these different types of primary source are illustrated on the following pages.

Secondary sources, by contrast, are almost always in either written or pictorial form. They are usually, but not always, produced at some time (often a long time) after the event or period which they describe or portray. The writer of a secondary source, such as a social and economic history of Britain, may use primary sources as well as secondary sources to describe events which happened long ago.

The Evening Poſt.

Numb. 1868.

From Tueſday July 18. to Thurſday July 20. 1721.

Since our laſt arriv'd one Mail from Holland, and one from France.

From the Supplement to the Amſterdam Gazette, July 25.

Genoa, July 5.

THE French Envoy Mſ. de Chavigny re-turn'd hither on the 29th of laſt Month, and on the 1ſt Inſt. had an Audience of the Doge. Both our Regency and the Mi-niſter of Great Britain, ſeem inclin'd to refer to the Mediation of that Envoy, the Pretenſions of the Engliſh on Account of the Sums which they ſay are due to them by ſome of our Merchants. Seeing the Britiſh Men of War which block up our Port, and were two Days ago reinforced by two more, have not as Yet made any Repriſals, there is Grounds to hope thoſe Differences will be adjuſted, by the friendly Offices of that Miniſter.

Montpelier, July 4. Tho' we are free from Contagion, ſuch Diſpoſitions are making, as may be of Uſe, in caſe we ſhould be viſited with it. All the Inhabitants of Boutonet, a ſmall Village contiguous to this City, have been turn'd out of their Houſes, which in caſe of need, will be uſed for Infirmiaries. Our Biſhop aſſiſts daily at the Council of Health, and has declar'd publickly, that if the Plague reaches this City, he will not only ſell all his Plate, Furni-ture, &c. but alſo expend his whole Income for Relief of the Sick. That moreover all the firſt Floor of his Palace ſhall be furniſh'd for Lodgings for the Prieſts, and other Perſons attending upon the Patients, whom he will Supply with Victuals and other Neceſſaries, that he will remove to the ſecond and take no Thought for himſelf till he has provided for the Neceſſities of others.

Milan, July 2. They write from Rome that an Expreſs from Scotland diſpatched by the Adherents of the Pretender, brought a Letter for the Pope, by which they in very Sub-miſſive Terms entreat the Holy Father, to follow the com-mendable Example of his Predeceſſor, and protect a forſaken Prince, aſſuring the Pope, that both he and they will always expreſs their Gratitude for it, of which they will give real Proofs if ever that Perſon ſhould recover his Dominions. Whereupon the Sacred Colledge was conven'd, and that Letter read to them by Cardinal Piazza, who repreſented to them on the Part of the Pope, that the Interceſſion of the Scots in behalf of the Pretender, the powerful Recom-mendation of the late Pope on his Death Bed, and the In-tereſt of the Roman Religion, require that a Prince, who is unfortunate on Account of his Religion, be ſupported in all Reſpects, and that for this Purpoſe His Holineſs deſigns not only, not to take off any thing of his former Allowance, but alſo to make an Addition to it, out of his own Privy Purſe. This at firſt was oppoſed, by the Cardinals, who alledg'd, that the Court of Rome did enough in confirming to him the Poſſeſſion of the Stately Palace the late Pope gran-ted him for his Reſidence, and protecting him openly againſt his Enemies, the Court of Madrid having, moreover, offer'd to bear Part of his Expences, and disburſt the Sums neceſſary for the ſame. However, in a Congregation held ſome time after about the ſame Affair, the Major Part of the Cardinals jump'd into the Pope's Opinion, on Condition, that the Subſidies ſhould not be drawn out of the Treaſure of Sixtus, becauſe neither the Sums borrowed from thence by the Spaniards on Pretence of a War with the Turks, nor thoſe granted to the Pretender to enable him to keep up a Royal Grandeur, have been made good again.

From the Hague Courant, July 25.

Leghorn, July 5. The Maſter of a French Ship has brought Letters from Tunis, dated the twenty firſt of laſt Month, importing, that the Rebellious Giarun Coggia, has defeated the Army of the Bey of Tripoly, and that the latter fearing the Conquerer ſhould force his Way into the City and get himſelf proclaim'd Bey, has ſent his whole Treaſure to Gerbi, intending to fly thither himſelf when he is no longer able to reſiſt.

From the Paris A-la main, July 26.

Paris, July 26. On the 22d Inſtant the King was ſome what indiſpoſed, but His Majeſty is now perfectly recover'd. On the 23d, the Duke de Aumont had an Appoplectick Fit, for which he was blooded twice, and took a Strong Vomit, 'tis much apprehended he can't recover: 'Tis much talked that the Arch Biſhop of Cambray receiv'd Advice Yeſter-day from Rome, of his being promoted to the Purple.

Hamburg, July 22.

The Muſcovite Reſident here has received an Expreſs with Advice, that the Ruſſian General in his late Expediti-on againſt Sweden landed abundance of Coſſacks, who ra-vaged and burnt on the Sea ſide near 590 Villages and Ma-nors, and deſtroy'd 12 Iron works. Juſt now a Report is ſpread here, that the King of Sweden is dead, but this News is not credited.

Briſtol, July 17. Yeſterday arrived here the George and Francis from Barbadoes; and juſt now arrived the Oldbury from Monſerat.

London, July 20.

Yeſterday Morning about 3, Sir Jonathan Trelawrey, Bart. Lord Biſhop of Wincheſter departed this Life, at his Palace at Chelſea. He was in Nov. 1685 Conſecrated Bi-ſhop of Briſtol, in March 1688-9, tranſlated from Briſt l to Exeter, and confirmed April 13, 1689; and in June 1707. he was Tranſlated to the See of Wirtor. He was one of the 7 Biſhops that were ſent to the Tower. His Lordſhip is ſuc-ceeded in his Honour of Baronet by his Eldeſt Son, now Sir John Trelawney, Member of Parliment for Leskard in Cornwall.

Extract from a newspaper - The Evening Post - published in July 1721

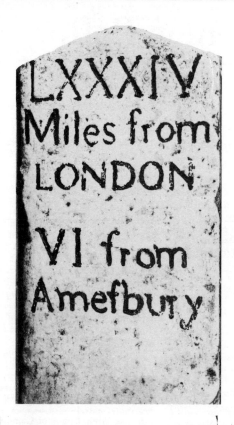

Eighteenth-century milestone at the side of a road in Wiltshire

Short extract from the handwritten diary of John Cabbell, describing a Grand Tour of Europe from Glasgow to Italy in 1833

high glee, at the pleasant prospect of a speedy termination to the voyage, on the 24th however to our great mortification, the wind gradually veered round to the N.E. from which quarter it blew a perfect gale, and set in a tremendously heavy sea — any thing but comfortable — Still, notwithstanding all these disadvantages, we made the passage in 52 hours the former passage had been accomplished in 38 hours & half which was uncommonly quick. 25th Arrived in Edinburgh at 9 — breakfasted at the London and started at 11, in a perfect purgatory of a Coach, six inside, oh! it was a sad squeeze, and along the most miserable country possible, the road most excessively dull — The inventor of six inside Coaches ought to be wellesqueezed, well, arrived in Old Glasgow at 4 OClock, quite delighted to find myself at home, in the midst of friends and of every comfort — after a very delightful trip of nearly six months, the

FRONTISPIECE TO MAVOR'S SPELLING BOOK

London, Published by LONGMAN, REES & C.º Sept. 1828.

Frontispiece to a school book published in 1836, illustrated with engravings of a dame school and two schools run by schoolmasters

THE

ENGLISH SPELLING-BOOK,

ACCOMPANIED BY

A PROGRESSIVE SERIES

OF

EASY AND FAMILIAR LESSONS,

INTENDED AS

AN INTRODUCTION

TO THE

READING AND SPELLING

OF

THE ENGLISH LANGUAGE.

By WILLIAM MAVOR, LL. D.

Four Hundred and Twenty-first Edition, Revised and Improved.

LONDON:
PRINTED FOR
LONGMAN, REES, ORME, BROWN, GREEN, AND LONGMAN,
PATERNOSTER-ROW,
AND TO BE HAD OF ALL BOOKSELLERS IN TOWN AND COUNTRY.
With a full and liberal Allowance to Schools.
Price Eighteenpence, Bound.

1836.

WASHING-DAY REFORM.

BANISH the antiquated, absurd, and destructive process of rubbing and boiling the clothes, and adopt the easy common-sense plan with

HARPER TWELVETREES'
VILLA WASHING MACHINE, £2 15s. (CASH PRICE £2 10s.)

OR WITH WRINGER AND MANGLER COMBINED, £5 5s. (CASH PRICE, £4 15s.,)
Which s the Gem of all Washing Machines and does the Fortnight's Family Wash in Four Hours

without Rubbing or Boiling, saving Five Hours of Copper Firing every Washing-day, as certified by Thousands of delighted "House-Mothers."

Mrs. WHITEWELL, Railway Cottage, Willesden, writes—"Your Villa Washer and Mangler is a wonderful machine. My daughter, aged fifteen, now does the washing for our family of twelve, in five hours, without any woman to help. We always used to have a woman two days."

Mrs. JONES, 16, Belgrave Gardens, Dover—"By following your printed directions in every detail, our washing, which formerly occupied a whole day is now easily done in two hours."

Mrs. TURNER, Fant, Maidstone—"I never thought anything could be half so useful. We have no trouble, and get our washing done in three hours, which before took a woman a whole day; and now we do without the washerwoman."

Carriage paid; free trial; easy instalment payments, or 10 per cent. cash discount. Illustrated Prospectus, 48 pp., from HARPER TWELVETREES, Laundry Machinist, 80, Finsbury Pavement, London, E.C. Works: Burdett Road, Bow, E.

Advertisement for a washing machine, published in 1897 in a cookery book called Tasty Dishes

Cartoon from the early
days of motoring,
published in Punch on
6 January 1904

Photograph of
Lancashire 'pit lasses
and pitboys' in 1920

In practice, it is sometimes difficult to say whether something is a primary source or a secondary source, unless you are given plenty of information about when, where, why, and how the source was first created. For instance, the sentence 'The crowd listened in silence; you could have heard a pin drop', sounds as though it might have been written at the time of the event it is describing. But it could just as easily have been written a hundred years later. A picture may look as if it was drawn on the spot but it could have been drawn many years later by an artist in a studio!

Checklist — Historical Evidence

Here are some of the checkpoints you can go through when you see a historical source for the first time.

1   *Can you understand the source? What does it tell you about the past?*

2   *Does it contain abbreviations you have never come across before, references to events or people you do not understand, or words and phrases which we no longer use?*

3   *What type of evidence is it – e.g. a diary entry, a letter, an official report, a book, a cartoon, a photograph? You can read descriptions of the main types of historical evidence you are most likely to see on pages 47–103.*

4   *Where does the source come from? Can it be trusted? (If you do not know its origin this does not necessarily mean that the source cannot be trusted. We often get information from newspaper articles and reports written by anonymous writers.)*

5   *When was the source created? Was it created within minutes, hours, days, weeks, months, or years of the event or happening it portrays?*

6   *Is there any statement, or clue, to show that the source is actually based on the writer's own experience or on events which he or she witnessed? In other words, was the writer in a good position to say what happened?*

7   *If the source was written a long time after the event, is there any reason to doubt the accuracy of the facts recalled by the writer?*

8   *Is it a primary or a secondary historical source?*

9   *Was there any particular reason why the source was written? Was it written to justify the writer's actions?*

10 *Are the facts in the source supported by facts you know about from other historical sources?*

Going through the Checklist

Here are two examples of the checklist in action. Notice how checkpoints are ignored if they do not apply to the extract in question.

Source A is taken from an article by an anonymous writer. Anonymous means that we do not know the writer's name. The article was published in a magazine called *The Quarterly Review* in the same year in which George Stephenson's *Locomotion* pulled the world's first trainload of passengers on the Stockton and Darlington Railway (27 September 1825).

SOURCE A

Can anything be more ridiculous than the prospect held out of locomotives travelling twice as fast as stage-coaches? We trust that Parliament will, in all railways it may sanction, limit the speed to eight miles an hour, which is as great as can be ventured on with safety.

The Quarterly Review, 1825

An exact replica of
Locomotion *runs today
on a railway line at the
Beamish Museum in
County Durham*

1 *Can you understand the source? What does it tell you about the past?*

The source tells us that some people were afraid of the new steam railway engines when they were first introduced. In many cases this was because they had a financial interest in coaching (such as ownership of a coaching inn or membership of a turnpike trust). They were afraid of the competition offered by the railways rather than their speed. The source also tells us that Parliament had to approve the building of each new railway. (Note that a speed of eight miles an hour is roughly the same as twelve kilometres an hour – slower than a bicycle!)

2 *Does it contain abbreviations you have never come across before, references to events or people you do not understand, or words and phrases which we no longer use?*

No.

3 *What type of evidence is it – e.g. a diary entry, a letter, an official report, a book, a cartoon, a photograph?*

It is written evidence from an article in a magazine.

4 *Where does the source come from? Can it be trusted?*

It was written by an anonymous writer for a magazine called *The Quarterly Review*. Since the article expresses opinions rather than facts it is not really necessary to consider whether the source can be trusted or not.

5 *When was the source created?*

In 1825.

6 *Is there any statement, or clue, to show that the source is actually based on the writer's own experience or on events which he or she witnessed? Was the writer in a good position to say what happened?*

Since we do not know who wrote the extract, we have no way of knowing for certain that it was based on the writer's own experience (i.e. of stage coaches). It seems reasonable to assume that it was.

7 *If the source was written a long time after the event is there any reason to doubt the accuracy of the facts recalled by the writer?*

This does not apply since the source was written in 1825.

8 *Is it a primary or a secondary historical source?*

It is a primary source. It was written in the year in which the Stockton and Darlington Railway was opened.

9 *Was there any particular reason why the source was written? Was it written to please or to annoy anyone? Was it written to justify the writer's actions?*

It was written to try to persuade Parliament to limit the speed of the new railway locomotives to the speed of a stage coach!

10 *Are the facts in the source supported by facts you know about from other historical sources?*

This does not apply since these are the writer's *opinions* – not facts which can be checked.

Source B comes from the introduction to a book called *The Farmer's Kalendar*. It was written by Arthur Young, a self-styled expert on farming, who by 1771 had been farming unsuccessfully for eight years but whose books on farming sold well. He did much to promote new and better ways of farming in the late eighteenth and early nineteenth centuries. In this extract he attacked the ideas of Jethro Tull which were first published in the book which you can see below. *The Farmer's Kalendar* was published in 1771 and was advertised as being 'BY AN EXPERIENCED FARMER'. Its main purpose was to tell farmers what jobs they should be doing on the farm in each month of the year.

Horſe-Hoeing Husbandry:

O R,

An ESSAY on the PRINCIPLES

O F

Vegetation *and* Tillage.

Deſigned to introduce

A NEW METHOD of CULTURE;

WHEREBY

The Produce of Land will be increaſed, and the
uſual Expence leſſened.

Together with

Accurate DESCRIPTIONS and CUTS of the Inſtruments
employed in it.

By J E T H R O   T U L L, *Eſq;*
Of Shalborne *in* Berkſhire.

The THIRD EDITION, very carefully Corrected.

To which is prefixed,

A New PREFACE by the EDITORS, addreſſed to all
concerned in AGRICULTURE.

L O N D O N:

Printed for A. MILLAR, oppoſite to *Catharine-ſtreet*
in the *Strand.*

M.DCC.LI.

Frontispiece to Jethro Tull's Horse-Hoeing Husbandry

SOURCE B

About fifty years ago, a celebrated Englifhman, Mr Tull, made many experiments, in a new method of culture, the great defign of which was to fet afide the ufe of manures. To this day he has had many followers. With the gentlemen that purfue his fyftem, tillage alone is neceffary – the plough is all in all, and nothing is to be dunged, or otherwife dreffed, but meadows or paftures. Were fuch ideas to become general, it is inconceivable how much mifchief they would occafion; for there cannot be more falfe principles, than thofe whereon they are built. Throughout thefe fheets, care is taken to keep clear fuch errors. The great importance of manures is duly attended to, and the farmer well inftructed how to raife as much as poffible himfelf.

1 *Can you understand the source? What does it tell you about the past?*

Arthur Young attacks Jethro Tull's theory ('false principles') that it is not necessary to manure fields which are used for growing crops. Jethro Tull was one of the pioneers of the new farming methods which were coming into use in the seventeenth and eighteenth centuries. He invented the seed drill which enabled farmers to drill (sow) their corn seed in rows. This was so that they could hoe in between the rows of young plants in the spring in order to increase yields of corn in the autumn. Hoeing got rid of the weeds. Jethro Tull argued that this meant there was no need to spread manure. Arthur Young thought that this was complete nonsense.

2 *Does it contain abbreviations you have never come across before, references to events or people you do not understand, or words and phrases which we no longer use?*

Arthur Young uses a number of farming expressions such as 'tillage' (land that is cultivated) and 'dunged' (manured) which you may not know. The most unusual thing about the extract, however, is the use of the old-fashioned letter 'f' in place of the letter 's' except when 's' is the last letter in a word. Many printers stopped using this method of spelling in about 1800. If you ever see a passage written like this there is always a good chance that it will have been written before 1800.

3 *What type of evidence is it – e.g. a diary entry, a letter, an official report, a book, a cartoon, a photograph?*

It is an extract from the introduction to a book.

4 *Where does the source come from? Can it be trusted?*

The Farmer's Kalendar was published in 1771. The extract records Arthur Young's opinion on the subject of manures, so the question of trusting whether he is right or wrong does not arise.

5   *When was the source created?*

It was written in about 1770 or 1771.

6   *Is there any statement, or clue, to show that the source is actually based on the writer's own experience or on events which he or she witnessed? Was the writer in a good position to say what happened?*

It was written 'BY AN EXPERIENCED FARMER'.

8   *Is it a primary or a secondary historical source?*

It is a primary source.

9   *Was there any particular reason why the source was written? Was it written to please or to annoy anyone? Was it written to justify the writer's actions?*

It was written to influence other farmers and to make money for its author.

Checkpoints 7 and 10 do not apply.

EXERCISES AND ACTIVITIES

Read the following extracts from the diary of Joseph Farington, a famous painter who was well known for the pictures he drew and painted on his many tours of Britain. In 1801 he visited Cromford in Derbyshire where Sir Richard Arkwright had built the world's first spinning mill (using water power) in 1771.

SOURCE A

August 22 1801 – In the evening I walked to Cromford & saw the Children coming from their work out of one of Mr Arkwright's Manufactories. I was glad to see them look in general very healthy and many with fine, rosy complexions. These children had been at work from 6 or 7 oclock this morning, & it was now near or abt. 7 in the evening. The time allowed them for resting is at 12 oclock 40 minutes during which time they dine. One of them, a Boy of 10 or 11 years of age, told me His wages were 3s 6d [18p] a week, & a little girl said Her wages were 2s 3d [11p] a week.

The author went to the chapel in Cromford the next day, Sunday, and saw boys from the factory in the congregation.

SOURCE B

August 23 – These children are employed in Mr Arkwright's work in the week-days, and on Sundays attend a school where they receive education. They came to Chapel in regular order and looked healthy & well & were decently cloathed & clean. They were attended by an Old Man their School Master. – To this school girls also go for the same purpose, and alternately with the Boys go to Church the Boys on one Sunday – the girls on the next following. – Whichever are not at Chapel are at the School, to which they both go every Sunday both morning and afternoon. The whole plan appears to be such as to do Mr Arkwright great credit.

1 *Use the checklist printed on page 9 to check through these two sources.*

2 *How many hours a week did the children actually work in the mill at Cromford? How much education did they receive in a year?*

3 *Can you think of a good reason why the children may have appeared 'very healthy and many with fine, rosy, complexions' even though they worked long hours in the mill?*

4 *Why would it be unwise to take this account (a) as evidence that Mr Arkwright was or was not a model employer, (b) as evidence that factory working conditions in the early years of the Industrial Revolution were not as bad as they are often painted? What else would you want to find out?*

5 *In what ways were girls not treated equally with boys (a) by Mr Arkwright, (b) by Mr Farington?*

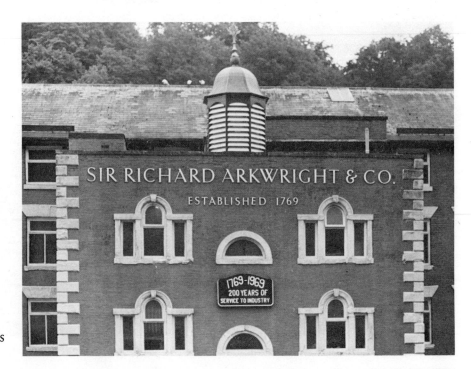

Arkwright's second cotton mill at Cromford, which was opened in 1783

HAS THE EVIDENCE BEEN ALTERED?

Most of the historical evidence that you will see will probably have been altered in some way. Look at the pair of pictures below of the town of Kendal in Cumbria (then in Westmorland). The pictures come from different editions of the same book – a collection of engravings of the Lake District. How has the second picture been altered? What change took place in Kendal in the ten years between 1835 and 1845?

Engraving of Kendal in a book published in about 1835

Engraving of Kendal in a new edition of the same book published in about 1845

Almost all the extracts you see will form only a very small part of a much bigger whole, such as a small paragraph taken from a newspaper of thirty-two pages, or a few sentences from a 600-page book.

Sometimes the text of the extract may have been altered to make it easier for you to read. Extra punctuation may have been added. Old spellings may have been corrected. Words we no longer use may have had their nearest modern meanings inserted into the extract – often inside square brackets to set them apart from ordinary curved brackets.

In many cases large parts of an extract will have been left out simply because there is not enough space to include the whole of the extract in a book, on an examination paper, or in a collection of historical documents. Often the intervening words and sentences are left out because they are difficult to understand today, irrelevant, or just boring! Missing text is sometimes shown by a row of dots like this: ... This is called an ellipsis (or ellipses if more than one). It is usually impossible to tell whether the dots show that just one or two words are missing or whether they indicate that several pages have been left out. In many extracts the ellipses will not be shown, since their inclusion every time a word, phrase, sentence, or paragraph is omitted would make the text unreadable.

EXERCISES AND ACTIVITIES

Many important documents and historical records have been destroyed by accident (such as in a fire) or by people who were ignorant of (or could not have known of, or suspected) their later importance (such as the childhood diaries of a future world leader). Undoubtedly some documents have been destroyed in order to conceal the truth. Only rarely do we have actual proof of this.

Here is an example, taken from the diary of Frances Stevenson, the secretary and mistress of David Lloyd George. He was the British prime minister during the First World War and had been involved in a row with General Maurice in 1918. The General claimed that Lloyd George misled the House of Commons by quoting inaccurate statistics about the number of troops fighting on the Western Front. Lloyd George successfully denied this in Parliament. Frances Stevenson recalled these events when she wrote this entry in her diary sixteen years later at a time when she was helping Lloyd George to write his memoirs of the First World War.

David Lloyd George

Frances Stevenson

October 5th 1934

Have been reading up the events connected with the Maurice Debate in order to help D. [David Lloyd George] with this Chapter in Vol. V, and am uneasy in my mind about an incident which occurred at the time & which is known only to J.T. Davies & myself. D. obtained from the W.O. [War Office] the figures which he used in his statement on April 9th in the House of Commons on the subject of manpower. These figures were afterwards stated by Gen. Maurice to be inaccurate. I was in J.T. Davies' room a few days after the statement, & J.T. was sorting out red dispatch boxes to be returned to the Departments. As was his wont, he looked in them before locking them up & sending them out to the Messengers. Pulling out a W.O. box he found in it, to his great astonishment, a paper from the D.M.O. [Department of Military Operations] containing modifications & corrections of the first figures they had sent, & by some mischance this box had remained unopened. J.T. & I examined it in dismay, & then J.T. put it in the fire, remarking, 'Only you and I, Frances, know of the existence of this paper.'

Frances Stevenson, *Lloyd George: A Diary*, edited by A. J. P. Taylor, Hutchinson, 1971

1 *Go through the checklist on page 9.*

2 *Who were J.T. and D., and what were the D.M.O. and the W.O.?*

3 *Why did J.T. put the document in the fire?*

4 *Why was J.T. incorrect in saying that 'Only you and I, Frances, know of the existence of this paper'? Who else must have known that it existed?*

5 *How likely do you think it is that Frances Stevenson would have been able to recall J.T.'s exact remarks over sixteen years after they were made?*

6 *How is this incident a warning to historians?*

FACT OR OPINION?

Events in the past are historical facts because historians have evidence to prove that the events actually happened. Historians always need proof. In many ways they are like lawyers in a law court. They obtain evidence from witnesses. They examine exhibits. They argue. They reach a conclusion or verdict. In a court of law, the judge and the jury try to decide the case on the basis of the facts not the opinions. So, too, do historians. When the members of a jury reach a decision on the basis of those facts they express an opinion themselves. Most times they are probably right. Sometimes they are wrong. So it is, too, with historians.

Sometimes it is difficult to tell if a statement is fact or opinion. It may be written as if it is a fact. If you know little about the subject you will probably have to accept it as such, unless it is clear that the statement could never be proved or disproved to everyone's satisfaction. For instance, if you read this statement quickly – 'The Victorian middle classes were deeply religious' – you will probably read it as a statement of fact rather than as a statement of an opinion. The writer does not say '*In my opinion* the Victorian middle classes were deeply religious'. Nonetheless, it is an opinion.

In the first place, we cannot be sure exactly who the writer means when he talks about the 'middle classes'. Does he include teachers? Or shopkeepers? In the second place, the phrase 'deeply religious' means different things to different people. To some it may mean a strict way of life with family prayers every day. To others it may mean going to a place of worship once a week.

Checklist — Facts and Opinions

Use your common sense if you are asked to say whether you think part of an extract is an opinion rather than a fact. Ask yourself:

1　*Which parts of the statement can probably be proved right or wrong? A specific statement, such as the name of a person or place, a date, number, or quantity, is something which can be proved, or disproved, as a fact. Either the name, place, date, number, or quantity is correct or it is not. The same thing applies to specific events or happenings which can also be easily proved or disproved. Either they did happen or they did not. This is a question of fact and not of opinion.*

2　*Which parts of the statement are obviously opinions and not facts? You can often detect opinions where the writer uses words which have no precise meaning, such as popular, beautiful, deeply, friendly, unpleasant, ugly, and unwise. By contrast many words, such as French-speaking, blue, fifty, and baker, have factual meanings.*

Bear in mind that opinions are often very useful to a historian because they show what people felt about an issue, or an event in the past. But beware of thinking that opinions are facts simply because you agree with them!

Going through the Checklist

'A Scottish piper leading a column of marchers with their banner inscribed "From Scotland to London": a scene on the road between Aylesbury and Berkhamsted.' The Illustrated London News, 29 October 1932.

Read the following extract and then go through the checklist. The extract is taken from an article written for a daily newspaper at the time of the Great Depression in the early 1930s. Social welfare benefits were inadequate at that time. Many people were poor and hungry.

It is difficult to recall any demonstration in Hyde Park during recent years that has touched the imagination of the onlookers more than did the march of the unemployed today. The crowd showed most interest in the men who walked with haversacks on their shoulders and boots or other oddments hanging from their haversacks, but its sympathy increased as the local men came by, men in a great many cases of poor physique, with pale, pinched faces and a look of worry in their eyes – young men with the stamp of despair on them and elderly men beside whom the hunger-marchers, chosen for their powers of endurance, looked fresh and vigorous.

Manchester Guardian, Friday, 28 October 1932

1   *Which parts of the statement can probably be proved right or wrong?*

That there was a march of the unemployed on 27 October 1932 in front of a crowd in Hyde Park is almost certainly a fact, since it can obviously be confirmed from other sources. That some of the men carried haversacks on their shoulders with boots and other oddments hanging from them is also a factual statement. They either did or they did not. If the writer had said that the crowd 'cheered or applauded as the local men came by' we could also accept this as a fact as well. As the text is written, however, we cannot be certain that this is what he means when he says 'its sympathy increased'.

2   *Which parts of the statement are obviously opinions and not facts?*

Phrases such as 'poor physique', 'pale, pinched faces', 'fresh and vigorous', 'a look of worry in their eyes', and 'the stamp of despair on them' mean different things to different people. A supporter of the government (which had been instrumental in aggravating the problems of the unemployed) might have disagreed with these descriptions. So we have to treat them as opinions and not as facts.

Overall, of course, the opinions expressed by the writer in this extract are invaluable. They give us a vivid demonstration of the impact that the Great Depression of the early 1930s had on the unemployed. The extract (opinion) makes a far greater effect than the statistic (fact) which tells us that 2 745 000 people were unemployed in Great Britain in 1932. Nonetheless, the impression we get is one that is based on opinions rather than on facts. We have to bear in mind that writers of vivid descriptions may sometimes exaggerate in order to make their descriptions colourful and lively.

EXERCISES AND ACTIVITIES

Read this extract carefully and then answer the questions which follow.

Industrial Pollution

Widnes is picturesque by the excess of its ugliness. Squalid cottages, large areas of muddy waste, with a pigstye here and there, and perhaps a gypsy's van in a desert of puddles and mud; black alleys, intricate gangways over an intricate network of railways, high chimneys on every side, and below these such grotesque shapes of towers and bubbling cauldrons, and tanks and wheels, as seems the very nightmare of industrialism. There are open sewers, too, through which the green liquid refuse of factories is carried off.

R.H. Sherard, *Pearson's Magazine*, 1896

1   *Which words in the extract have no precise meaning?*

2   *Which parts of the statement can probably be proved right or wrong?*

3   *Which parts of the statement are obviously opinions and not facts?*

4   *What is the value of an extract like this? Compare it with the photograph of a chemical works in the nearby town of Northwich in Cheshire taken about twelve years earlier.*

Chemical works at Northwich in Cheshire in 1884

ACCURACY AND RELIABILITY

Most of the extracts which you will see will be far too short for you ever to say with confidence that they are trustworthy and reliable sources of information. On the other hand you may be able to detect mistakes or inaccuracies in an extract which throw some doubt on the reliability of the historical source from which the extract is taken.

Checklist — **Accuracy and Reliability**

Ask yourself these questions.

1 *Are there any obvious mistakes or errors of fact in the extract? We can often test for mistakes by comparing one historical source with another. If there are mistakes it does not necessarily mean that the rest of the source is inaccurate. Nor does it mean that the source has no value. But it does mean that you should exercise some caution in treating the rest of the source as a reliable source of information.*

2 *Have you any reason to think that the facts quoted in the account may give a distorted view of the events which actually occurred?*

3 *Has the author left out any obvious facts which tell a different story from the one conveyed by the extract? Is there any reason to think that they were left out deliberately? (It may be that the author was just unaware or ignorant of these facts or could not have known about them anyway.)*

4 *Has the author used any words or phrases which show that he or she approves or disapproves of a person, an action, or an event? Does the author show any signs of being biased or prejudiced (see pages 27–35)?*

Going through the Checklist

Source A which follows is an extract from a biography of Lloyd George which was first published in 1954. We can test the accuracy and reliability of this statement about the suffragettes by comparing the facts in this extract with those in newspapers published in June 1913 at the time of the incident which it describes (Sources B to F).

SOURCE A

SUFFRAGETTES

The most determined martyr of them all, Miss Emily Davidson, red-haired, green-eyed, half-demented girl, denied the sacrifice of her life when she leapt from an upper floor in Holloway Prison after a hunger-strike, was killed in the end on Derby Day, 1913, when she flung herself under the flying hooves of the King's horse as it led the field, thundering round Tattenham Corner.

Frank Owen, *Tempestuous Journey: Lloyd George His Life and Times*, Hutchinson, 1954

SOURCE B

ABOYEUR'S DERBY

At Tattenham Corner, and after rounding it, he [Aboyeur] still maintained his place [as leader of the field]

The Times, Thursday, 5 June 1913

SOURCE C

NARRATIVES OF SPECTATORS
The general impression of those who saw the incident at close quarters seemed to be that the woman had seized hold of the first horse she could reach – which happened to be the King's – not with the intention of disqualifying any particular horse, but of interfering with and, if possible, spoiling the race as a whole.

The Times, Thursday, 5 June 1913

SOURCE D

AN EYEWITNESS
They had just got round the Corner and all had passed but the King's horse, when a woman squeezed through the railings and ran out into the course. She made straight for Anmer, and made a sort of leap for the reins. I think she got hold of them, but it was impossible to say.

An eyewitness account in the *Manchester Guardian*,
Thursday, 5 June 1913

SOURCE E

DEATH OF MISS DAVISON
Miss Emily Wilding Davison, the suffragist who interfered with the King's horse during the race for the Derby, died in hospital at Epsom at 4.50 yesterday afternoon.

The Times, Monday, 9 June 1913

SOURCE F

INQUEST ON EMILY WILDING DAVISON
(Tuesday, 10 June 1913)
Police-sergeant Bunn said he was about twenty yards [18 metres] away from Miss Davison when she rushed out on the course. 'I saw the woman throw her hands up in front of the horses. Some had previously passed her.'

The Coroner, in summing up, said he did not think that Miss Davison aimed at the King's horse in particular but that her intention was to upset the race. The jury would probably dismiss from their minds the idea that she intended to take her life.

The jury returned a verdict of 'Death by misadventure'.

The Suffragette, Friday, 13 June 1913

SOURCE G

Tombstone at Morpeth, Northumberland

1   *Are there any obvious mistakes or errors of fact in the extract (i.e. Source A)?*

Yes.

(a) The tombstone (Source G) shows clearly that her surname was Davison not Davidson.

(b) She died in hospital on Sunday, 8 June not on Derby Day itself – Wednesday, 4 June (Sources E and G).

(c) The King's horse (Anmer) did not lead the field at Tattenham Corner. The eventual winner, a horse called Aboyeur, was the leader (Source B).

2   *Have you any reason to think that the facts in the account may give a distorted view of the events which actually occurred?*

Yes. There is no evidence that 'she flung herself under the flying hooves of the King's horse'. Quite the contrary.

(a) Two of the sources (C and F) indicated that it was sheer accident that she was knocked down by the King's horse. In other words, she did not specifically select the King's horse in order to make her protest.

(b) Far from flinging herself *under* the horse, one eyewitness (Source D) said she made 'a sort of leap for the reins' and this was confirmed by a police officer at the inquest (Source F).

3   *Has the author left out any obvious facts which tell a different story from the one conveyed by the extract?*

Yes. The author describes her as 'The most determined martyr of them all' but fails to say that the inquest jury returned a verdict of 'Death by misadventure' (Source F).

4   *Has the author used any words or phrases which show that he or she approves or disapproves of a person, an action, or an event? Does the author show any signs of being biased or prejudiced (see pages 27–8)?*

Yes. The use of the phrase 'half-demented' is intended to suggest that Emily Davison was halfway towards being insane. This was not the verdict of the jury at the inquest (Source F). The use of adjectives such as 'red-haired' and 'green-eyed' can also be interpreted as indicating bias, since they are obviously intended to suggest that she was unbalanced, wilful, headstrong and envious of others. Nor was she a 'girl' (with its implication of inexperience and impetuousness). As you can see from her tombstone (Source G), she was a mature woman of 40 years of age.

EXERCISES AND ACTIVITIES

Look at the following accounts of the same incident (Sources H and I). Both are secondary sources. Test each carefully against the facts you have already noted in Sources B to G. Are these reports accurate and reliable accounts of the incident at the 1913 Derby?

SOURCE H

On Derby Day, 1913, Emily Davidson, a suffragette, threw herself in front of the King's horse and died next day.

G.D.H. Cole and Raymond Postgate,
The Common People, Methuen, 1963

SOURCE I

The most dramatic and most public gesture of the Suffragette campaign occurred on June 4, 1913, when Emily Wilding Davison threw herself in front of the horses as they rounded Tattenham Corner in the Derby. She brought down the King's horse *Anmer*, and injured herself so severely that she died in hospital a few days later.

James Bishop, *Social History of Edwardian Britain*,
Angus and Robertson, 1977

BIAS AND PREJUDICE

Bias in history presents one side of the picture only, such as setting out only those arguments you agree with or listing only the good or bad points (but not both). It may exaggerate or distort what someone has done or said.

An advertisement is an obvious example of bias. It does not tell you the bad points about a product. Nor does it tell you about better products from other manufacturers!

Similar bias can be found in both primary and secondary historical sources. People often gloss over, or ignore, bad points and the other side of an argument. They may select only those facts which support their case. They may use words designed to make readers feel strongly either for or against a particular point of view. Bias is often political or religious.

A historian must study evidence carefully to see if it is biased in any way. If there is bias, it does not mean the source is valueless. Far from it. The source may be valuable precisely because it reveals the attitudes of a large group of people. It shows how people felt and thought at the time.

Prejudice is an extreme form of bias. Prejudice does not listen to reason. Prejudice can be suspected if a writer is known to have, or reveals, a hatred, dislike, or an unreasonable attitude to particular people or places. This can sometimes happen, even in the writings of well-known historians. Political or religious beliefs, for instance, can sometimes lead to a very biased selection of evidence and lead the writer to a faulty conclusion. Prejudice can often be seen in writings about:

- a particular race of people (e.g. the Arabs or the Jews)
- a particular nation (e.g. the Soviet Union or the United States)
- a person – particularly one with controversial opinions, such as Karl Marx, the founder of modern communism
- the part played by women in society or in politics
- a political party (e.g. Communist, Socialist, Conservative)
- a class of people (e.g. upper, middle, or working class)
- a minority group
- a religion
- a way of life (e.g. that of the gypsies).

Bias and prejudice can be expressed in pictures as well, such as in pictures which caricature ethnic groups and foreigners.

You may be able to understand, or even appreciate, why there is bias – like the bias in favour of Napoleon by a French historian and the bias in favour of Nelson or Wellington by a British historian. Nonetheless, it is still bias.

If you see or suspect bias in a historical extract you should treat the whole of the extract with caution. The writer may have allowed bias to alter the way in which certain facts are chosen and other facts left out.

Checklist — **Bias and Prejudice**

Study the source carefully. If possible, compare the facts in the extract with other evidence, including engravings and photographs.

1 *Which words, phrases, and sentences seem to you to be opinions rather than facts (see pages 19–23)?*

2 *Are these opinions based on all the facts or only on certain facts which support the opinion in question?*

3 *Does anything in the extract contradict facts which you already know to be true?*

4 *Does the writer appear to take sides by presenting only one side of an argument or by showing only one side in a favourable or unfavourable light?*

5 *Is any part of the extract an obvious lie or exaggeration?*

6 *Has the writer used colourful words or phrases to try to influence the way you feel about the facts? For instance, an action may be described as being 'brave' or 'courageous' in one writer's view and 'foolhardy' or 'irresponsible' in an opposing view.*

7 *Are any of the statements controversial? This means anything with which some other people are almost certain to disagree.*

Going through the Checklist

These examples refer to the 'Bloody Sunday' demonstration in Trafalgar Square on Sunday, 13 November 1887.

Contemporary drawing by W.B. Wollen showing the Life Guards patrolling Trafalgar Square on 'Bloody Sunday', 13 November 1887

SOURCE A

LONDON 1887

November. The subject which most commands interest just now is the battle of Trafalgar Square on Sunday 13 November. The so-called 'unemployed' & a good contingent of roughs had taken possession of the space round Nelson's Column in Trafalgar Square since the middle of October & had persistently slept there & held meetings assisted by the Socialists & the extreme Radicals . . . Sunday, 13th of November arrived, & some Radical & all the Socialist Clubs from all parts of the town set off, followed by the whole criminal population & vast numbers of sightseers, who came to see the fun, – for Trafalgar Square.

Extract from the Journals of Mary, Lady Monkswell,
A Victorian Diarist, edited by the Hon E.C.F. Collier,
1944

SOURCE B

In November 1887, Cunninghame Graham and Burns vainly attempted to storm Trafalgar Square against the police at the head of the unemployed; Alfred Linnell, the first English Socialist martyr, died of injuries received from the police in the conflict.

G.D.H. Cole and Raymond Postgate,
The Common People, Methuen, 1963

1   *Which words, phrases, and sentences seem to you to be opinions rather than facts (see pages 19–23)?*

EXAMPLE from Source A

The 'battle' of Trafalgar Square. Was it really a 'battle'?

EXAMPLE from Source B

The first English Socialist 'martyr'. Was he really a 'martyr'?

2   *Are these opinions based on all the facts or only on certain facts which support the opinion in question?*

EXAMPLE from Source B

'Alfred Linnell, the first English Socialist martyr, died of injuries received from the police in the conflict.' The authors do not tell us the Coroner's verdict on Linnell's death; nor do they say whether or not there was an official enquiry into his death. We might suspect bias here.

3   *Does anything in the extract contradict facts which you already know to be true?*

EXAMPLE from Source A

'The so-called "unemployed" '. The writer obviously does not believe that unemployment was a serious problem in London in 1887. Instead, she casts doubt on whether the 'unemployed' were genuinely unemployed. However, if you have studied this topic in detail you will have found that statistics and newspaper accounts show clearly that unemployment was indeed a serious problem in London in 1887 and one that caused considerable distress amongst the working classes (e.g. children were sent home from school for not paying their weekly penny fees). Lady Monkswell could have seen this for herself if she had read the issue of *The Illustrated London News* from which this picture comes. It was published just two weeks before 'Bloody Sunday'.

An engraving from The Illustrated London News, 29 October 1887: 'The Poor Helping the Poor: Scene in Trafalgar-Square at One a.m., Tuesday, October 18'. A group of poor people who were employed had collected £3 to buy 'sixty gallons of tea and coffee, and several hundred rations of bread and cheese, which were distributed in Trafalgar Square, during the small hours of the Tuesday morning, to a ravenously eager but perfectly orderly crowd of between four and five hundred persons'.

4 *Does the writer appear to take sides by presenting only one side of an argument or by showing only one side in a favourable or unfavourable light?*

EXAMPLE from Source A

The writer unfairly links the socialists and Radicals with the 'criminal' classes. She makes no attempt to explain why the socialists and Radicals took up the cause of the unemployed.

EXAMPLE from Source B

The writers are almost certainly left wing in their sympathies and take sides. They make no attempt to criticise the use of violence by the demonstrators. They call Alfred Linnell a 'Socialist martyr', although people from opposing political parties would be most unlikely to use the word 'martyr' in this context.

5 *Is any part of the extract an obvious lie or exaggeration?*

EXAMPLE from Source A

The phrase 'the whole criminal population'. The writer does not mean London's genuine criminals since only a few thieves would have bothered to attend a demonstration by poor people who were unemployed. Instead she uses the phrase as if to suggest that anyone supporting the unemployed must be a 'criminal'.

6 *Has the writer used colourful words or phrases to try to influence the way you feel about the facts?*

EXAMPLE from Source A

Use of the phrase 'a good contingent of roughs' further denigrates the people who supported the cause of the unemployed.

7 *Are any of the statements controversial?*

EXAMPLE from Source B

'Alfred Linnell, the first English Socialist martyr, died of injuries received from the police in the conflict.' This is almost certainly controversial, since it states as fact that Linnell died at the hands of the police. The authors do not attempt to examine the exact circumstances in which he died (which might or might not support the notion that Linnell was indeed a martyr).

EXERCISES AND ACTIVITIES

The following extracts describe an incident at Llanelli in August 1911 during the national railway strike. Keir Hardie, the author of Source A, was probably the leading figure in the early years of the Labour party. He was first elected to Parliament as an independent Labour member in 1892. David Lloyd George, the Chancellor of the Exchequer, was the most influential member of the Liberal government at that time. Winston Churchill (much later a Conservative prime minister) was then a member of the Liberal party and held the office of Home Secretary. As such he was responsible for the police and for maintaining law and order in England and Wales. It was Churchill who sent the troops to the railway stations during the strike. Randolph Churchill, the author of Source B, was Winston Churchill's son.

SOURCE A

As showing how the troops were likely to be used to shoot men down like dogs, take what happened at Llanelly. A train was stopped by a crowd of strikers squatting down on the line in front of it. Some troops, quartered at the station, rushed up at the double, and lined up on both sides of the engine . . . But for the presence of the soldiers nothing more would have happened. Some boys and youths did pelt stones at the soldiers, and one of them was struck. Mr Lloyd George spoke of what happened as being undoubtedly a 'very great riot,' and described the engine driver as lying bleeding and helpless from the violence of the mob. This, however, was all imagination without an atom of truth. The train was standing in a deep cutting, and the official story is that stones were coming in showers from both sides. Now, not one pane of glass in the carriage windows was broken, not one passenger was hurt or molested, in fact, they were looking out of the windows, no civilian was struck, no property was damaged; there was no riot. But the officer in command ordered the people to disperse; he gave them one minute in which to do so; at the end of the minute he ordered five shots to be fired which killed two men outright, and wounded four others. John Johns, one of the murdered men, was sitting on the garden wall of his own house in shirt and trousers, looking on; the other was also in his garden at the top of the railway embankment. No one has ever alleged that either of them threw stones or took any part in what little stone throwing there was. Presumably, however, they made good targets, and so were picked off. For the troops are not to fire at random. They are not to use blank cartridges, even by way of warning, they are not to fire over the heads of the people, they are not to fire at the legs of the crowd; their instructions were to make every shot tell, they were to shoot to kill . . . Hours afterwards when an infuriated crowd were looting, burning, and destroying railway stock, the Major and his men remained immovable until a wagon exploded and killed another four people.

J. Keir Hardie, *Killing No Murder*, 1911

SOURCE B

The railway strike was over, and, wonderful to relate, there was very little bloodshed. The troops fired, when they did fire with great caution and deliberation, usually over the heads of the crowds. Ironically, it was two days after the settlement of the strike that the only fatality from the use of troops occurred. This was at Llanelly, where four people were killed after a train had been held up by rioters, the engine driver had been knocked senseless and looting had begun. This calculated violence by the strikers exceeded anything which had occurred hitherto ...

For all the criticism that came Churchill's way from the Labour members of Parliament for his attitude to the use of troops during this strike, there is little doubt that the King's telegram [congratulating Churchill but regretting the 'unfortunate incident at Llanelly'] represented public opinion at the time.

Randolph S. Churchill, *Winston S. Churchill: Young Statesman 1901–1914*, Heinemann, 1967

'Rioting at Llanelly: The smashed windows of the troop train', The Graphic, 26 August 1911. Does this prove or disprove anything in either Source A or Source B?

1   Read through the extracts carefully and go through the checklists on pages 9 and 28 with each one.

2   Why would you immediately suspect that each author might be biased in his account of the incident? How does this affect the way you treat his description of the incident at Llanelli?

3   Which parts of these accounts do you think are (a) probably accurate and can be accepted as facts, (b) opinions rather than facts, (c) statements which may be exaggerated or even false, (d) biased or prejudiced in one direction or the other?

4   Which do you think are the worst examples of bias in these extracts?

5   Compare your answers with those of your friends. Can you be sure that your answer is unbiased?

6   Is it possible to think of any source that could have given an unbiased account of what happened at Llanelli?

7   *Were either of these writers eyewitnesses?*

8   *Is an account more or less likely to be biased if it was written by someone who was not actually an eyewitness? Or would it make no difference at all?*

9   *Have you enough information to decide for yourself what really happened at Llanelli in August 1911? What other sources might you wish to consult to confirm your opinion or to help you make a judgement?*

10   *Who was to blame for the loss of life at Llanelli? Was it (a) the strikers, (b) the soldiers, (c) the officer commanding the soldiers, (d) Winston Churchill, (e) the government, (f) the railway companies which held out against the strikers? Give your reasons.*

GAPS AND CONTRADICTIONS

As you have seen, historical sources, both primary and secondary, often contradict each other. Differences of opinion are bound to occur but sources also often disagree about the significance of important facts and events. They are sometimes inconsistent, even contradicting statements made earlier in the same document.

As you have also seen, a source will sometimes leave out inconvenient facts which do not support the opinions or claims of the writer. There may be large gaps in the records. But note that gaps in a source, such as missing days in a diary, can also occur for very simple reasons, such as absence or ill health.

Checklist — Gaps and Contradictions

Here are some of the pointers you can look out for.

1   *Does anything in the extract contradict facts which you know about from other sources? Be careful to distinguish between facts and opinions (see pages 19–23). The contradictions between sources may merely reflect different ways of looking at the same evidence. Emily Wilding Davison's actions at Epsom in 1913 (see pages 24–7) were those of a martyr in the eyes of fellow suffragettes and the actions of someone who was 'half-demented' in the eyes of government supporters.*

2   *Are there any gaps in the evidence – such as missing dates, facts, or personalities – which support a different version of the events recorded by the writer? If so, is there a good reason for this, such as illness or because these other facts were known only at a later date?*

3 *Is anything in the extract confusing? Does it contradict another part of the same document, for instance by mixing up dates, or people, or the sequence of events?*

4 *Does the writer seek to take credit for successes which other people claim for themselves? Equally, does the writer put the blame for failures on to other people?*

Going through the Checklist

Read through the following extracts from two long articles published about the London Dock Strike of 1889. The dockers had gone on strike demanding sixpence an hour – the 'dockers' tanner', as it was called. The strike was successful. They got the extra money and an improvement in working conditions. Their success gave a huge boost to the trade union movement in the 1880s. Two of the participants in the strike made a great name for themselves in the trade union and socialist movements. They were Ben Tillett, the author of Source A, and John Burns, the author of Source B.

Hiring dock labourers at the West India Docks, The Illustrated London News, 20 February 1886

SOURCE A

As secretary of the Dock Labourers' Union and the originator and organizer of the late strike I should like to tell my own story in my own way ... In the summer of 1887, after twelve years' service on the wharves, I left active work and became the secretary of the 'Tea Coopers and General Labourers' Association' [later called 'The

Dock Labourers' Union'] . . . The dock labourers as a class are so poor that the formation of the Union was a very difficult task. We managed, however, after great exertions to collect a band of about 2500 men.

A year later he had to leave his job for health reasons and membership of the Union fell.

However at the time of the strike we mustered 800. [On Monday, 12 August] a deputation came to me with a request that I would place the men's demands as drawn up by themselves before the dock officials, and ask that an answer should be given on the next day . . . On Wednesday, August 14th, a general strike was agreed upon, and after a meeting of the South Dock workers, a procession was formed and a visit paid to the gates of the other docks. The enthusiastic shouts of the men soon acted as a call to arms to those working within. From the woodyard of the West India Dock the workers came out in hundreds . . . We then marched to the East India Dock, and with added recruits proceeded to the Millwall Dock . . . On that day I addressed twelve meetings.

At six o'clock the following morning we were astir and found the ranks of the strikers largely increased. We marched our forces in procession to the West, East, South, Victoria and Albert Docks, and at each dock speeches were made by representatives of the men . . . On the third day of the strike we marched, with banners and brass bands, to the number of 10 000 through the City, and a deputation attended at the Dock House to discuss with the directors the points in dispute . . . It was during our march to the City on that morning that I first met John Burns, who together with Tom Mann proved such friends to us during the strike . . .

The suggestion that the strike was the work of socialists and politicians is as untrue as it is unfair to the cause of labour. Neither socialism, creed, nor politics entered into the strike. The credit of the victory is due to the men themselves, and not to any speech-making from outsiders.

Benjamin Tillett, *The English Illustrated Magazine*,
November 1889

Ben Tillett

John Burns

SOURCE B

It is now some six years since John Williams, myself, and others, commenced our crusade amongst the dockers ... We who were thus openly agitating and spreading discontent in this neglected corner of the world of labour ... deliberately set ourselves to make the men revolt against their lot.

... An old and settled dock hand, named Harris, appealed to me to form a permanent dock hands' trade union. I consented, and held a meeting of two thousand men, at which many men were enrolled. These were men who had refused to join the old dockers' union, which from one cause and another, had ceased to be worth its name. But the information of the new union forced the old into an activity which it had not theretofore displayed; and of this unwonted activity the immediate outcome was the strike in the South Dock on August 13th. Some 300 men came out, refusing to work any longer for 5d an hour.

On Wednesday, August 14th, Mr Mann went down, on a telegraphic summons, to address the men. On the day following I presented myself at the West India Docks, to render what help I could. Discontent was simmering; I spoke to the men, and found them eager and receptive ... This meeting of 4000 dockers I look back to as the real commencement of the Strike ... on Thursday, Friday, and Saturday, August 15th, 16th and 17th, I spoke thirty-six times – outside of wharves, docks and warehouses, Mr Mann, Mr Tillett, and Mr Champion did as much.

John Burns, *New Review*, October 1889

1   *Does anything in the extract contradict facts which you know about from other sources?*

Ben Tillett claims that he was 'the originator and organizer of the late strike' but John Burns gives the impression that he was responsible, and looked back to the meeting of 4000 dockers which he addressed on Thursday, 15 August as the 'real commencement of the Strike'. John Burns's statement is an opinion. Ben Tillett's claim is a fact – since he was secretary of the Dock Labourers' Union. But, on his own admission, the union had only 800 members at the start of the strike, while 10 000 dockers marched in procession just three days later.

2   *Are there any gaps in the evidence – such as missing dates, facts, or personalities – which support a different version of the events recorded by the writer?*

Ben Tillett says that on the third day of the strike (Friday) 10 000 strikers marched through the City of London, and that a deputation negotiated with the employers at Dock House. This was obviously a substantial protest march with 'banners and brass bands' and must have made an impression on Londoners. He also says 'It was during our march to the City on that morning that I first met John Burns ...'. Yet there is no mention of this meeting or of the procession in the account written by John Burns.

3   *Is anything in the extract confusing? Does it contradict another part of the
     same document, for instance by mixing up dates, or people, or the
     sequence of events?*

John Burns looked back on his meeting of 4000 dockers on Thursday,
15 August as 'the real commencement of the Strike' but earlier he says
that the strike began 'in the South Dock on August 13th. Some 300
men came out . . .'. Even this is contradicted by Ben Tillet who says
that, 'On Wednesday, August 14th a general strike was agreed upon,
and after a meeting of the South Dock workers, a procession was
formed . . .'.

4   *Does the writer seek to take credit for successes which other people
     claim for themselves? Equally, does the writer put the blame for failures
     on to other people?*

Both writers, understandably, seek to take credit for the success of the
strike – Ben Tillett as organiser of the Dock Labourers' Union, John
Burns as an outside agitator. Each gives the other some credit, but
only when coupled with the names of other supporters! Ben Tillett
gives credit as follows: 'John Burns, who together with Tom Mann
proved such friends to us during the Strike', but then he goes on to say
that the credit of the victory was due 'not to any speech-making from
outsiders'. This can only refer to men like John Burns!

John Burns also gives credit to his rival: 'Mr Mann, Mr Tillett and Mr
Champion did as much', but he also denigrates Tillett's union, 'which
from one cause and another, had ceased to be worth its name'!

EXERCISES AND ACTIVITIES

Read through the extracts from the articles by Ben Tillett and John Burns
again. Go through the checklist for yourself.

1   *What further gaps and contradictions can you find?*

2   *Sum up the ways in which the two accounts disagree. Do they disagree
     on matters of fact or on matters of opinion?*

3   *How important were the socialists to the strike (a) in Ben Tillett's view,
     (b) in John Burns's view?*

EYEWITNESSES AND HEARSAY EVIDENCE

Eyewitness evidence can take several different forms. A newspaper report, a broadcast, a diary, a photograph, a letter, a television news report, a newsreel film, and a drawing are just some of the different ways in which eyewitnesses have recorded the things they have actually seen or heard. In other words they have witnessed an event or happening with their own eyes and ears. Hence 'eyewitness'. Eyewitnesses can be mistaken but their evidence must be taken seriously if they were really in a position to see or hear something significant.

In a court of law, the evidence from an eyewitness is carefully examined by a judge and by lawyers. It is their job to test the reliability of the witness. They try to make sure that the evidence given is truthful, exact, and accurate. They test the witness to make sure that he or she was not mistaken.

In history we cannot question the eyewitnesses who tell us what happened in the past. But we can compare their evidence with other eyewitness accounts and with facts we know about from other sources. We can also use common sense. For instance, how likely is it that someone will have been able to remember the exact words of a conversation which took place fifty years earlier? We ask questions to test the reliability of the evidence to see if the eyewitness can really be believed. Was the eyewitness in a good position to see what happened?

Sometimes a source may give the impression that the writer was an eyewitness when in fact the evidence is really based on a report of the incident which the writer heard from someone else. This is called *hearsay evidence*. Witnesses are not usually allowed to use hearsay evidence in a court of law, since there may be no way of checking whether it is accurate. Hearsay evidence is sometimes used by historians, however with some reservations. This is because it may have been altered or misunderstood by the person who heard it in the first place. Nonetheless, hearsay evidence is often the only way we have of knowing what went on at a private or secret meeting. For example, you might see something like this in the memoirs of Green:

> I had a long conversation with Black on the 10th. She told me that Brown had stormed out of the Cabinet in a temper.

In other words, Black was the eyewitness *not* Green (i.e. assuming that Black was herself at the Cabinet meeting in question). It would be eyewitness evidence only if Green had been at the Cabinet meeting herself. Instead, it is hearsay evidence and cannot be entirely trusted since Black could have heard the report from White, and White could have heard it from Grey! We have no way of knowing for certain unless the report is backed up by evidence from another source.

A particular problem with eyewitnesses is the question of when they put their recollections down on paper for the first time or in some other permanent form. You can see a discussion of this in the section on pages 64–5, which deals with memoirs and oral history (spoken recollections of the past).

Although eyewitness evidence has many advantages, there is a danger in thinking that an eyewitness must know the truth, or that an eyewitness would not tell a lie. In fact, many eyewitnesses see only a small part of what actually happens. Their evidence is just as liable to bias or distortion as that of writers who were not on the scene at the time of the event.

Checklist — Evidence from Eyewitnesses

1   *Does the source indicate in any way that the eyewitness actually saw or experienced the events recorded? We can often find this out from the evidence itself. Look out for clues in the writing which suggest that the writer was actually present, such as the use of 'I' and 'me' – as in 'I saw', 'I heard', 'a women next to me', 'I tripped and fell'. Other statements may suggest strongly that the writer was an eyewitness, although they could have come from other sources, such as 'the crowd gasped', 'the smell was overpowering'.*

2   *Does the source indicate in any way that it is wholly or partly based on hearsay evidence?*

3   *Is there any clue to show that the eyewitness was in a good position to see what happened?*

4   *Does the evidence justify the actions of the eyewitness in any way? This does not mean that the evidence cannot be trusted, but it does show that the eyewitness is not impartial.*

5   *Are there any other reasons why we may need to treat the evidence of the eyewitness with caution?*

6   *Is there any way of confirming any of the facts described by the eyewitness?*

Going through the Checklist

Read the following extracts from a magazine article, 'The Agricultural Labourer', from a series entitled 'How the Other Half Lives'. In it the author records a conversation she had with the wife of a Dorset farmworker in about 1895.

A ROOM IN
A DORSETSHIRE
COTTAGE.

This picture illustrated H.G. Pearce's article in The English Illustrated Magazine *in 1895*

H.G. PEARCE:	It seems a nice cottage on the whole?
DORSET WOMAN:	Yes, ma'am, it's a very tidy one. There is this kitchen and a scullery and two bedrooms, and we pay 2s 6d [13p] a week rent; it has a good garden, too, you see. The worst of it is there is no water near except in that ditch outside, and that is often dried up in the summer. All our drinking water we have to fetch from the well in a neighbour's garden, a tidy step from here.

. . .

H.G. PEARCE:	Are wages pretty good here?
DORSET WOMAN:	My husband he works for that farmer who lives over there. He gets 11s [55p] a week now, but it will drop to 10s [50p], I expect, before very long; it generally does in the winter. Of course he gets more pay at harvest time; we generally buys our pig then. Some of the masters here object to their men keeping pigs – says it leads to dishonesty, but they allow them a piece of ground in one of their fields to grow potatoes on. Then, you see, it gets manured along with the rest of the field. The potato crop lasts from May to September, the bit of land is then returned to the farmer.

. . .

H.G. PEARCE:	How do you manage about food so far from any town?
DORSET WOMAN:	Well you see, we don't require much meat beyond bacon. The butcher he do come once a week of a Saturday night to his regular customers, but there is very little taken in this village. Rabbits are plentiful enough, and you can get one for Sunday's dinner at 4d [2p] or so. Coal was 1s 6d a cwt. [£1.50 a tonne] during the winter, it's 1s 3d [£1.25 a tonne] now. Bread we pay 5d [2p] a loaf. Oddments and groceries we can get at the village shop, but things do seem dear there. You see there is no one to say them 'nay', as you may say.

H.G. Pearce, *English Illustrated Magazine*,
1895

1 *Does the source indicate in any way that the eyewitness actually saw or experienced the events recorded?*

Obviously yes. But note that the eyewitness here is the writer, H.G. Pearce, *not* the Dorset woman.

2 *Does the source indicate in any way that it is wholly or partly based on hearsay evidence?*

No. The writer reports what she actually saw and heard herself from the lips of the farmworker's wife.

3 *Is there any clue to show that the eyewitness was in a good position to see what happened?*

Obviously yes – 'It seems a nice cottage on the whole?'.

4 *Does the evidence justify the actions of the eyewitness in any way?*

No.

5 *Are there any reasons why we may need to treat the evidence of the eyewitness with caution?*

It is always possible that the writer omitted comments which did not support the ideas expressed in her article. But this is also the case with many other historical sources. A writer obviously selects only the evidence which he or she thinks you should see.

6 *Is there any way of confirming any of the facts described by the eyewitness?*

We cannot confirm the specific facts quoted in the article, since they refer to one Dorset household only. But we could compare this account with similar descriptions of rural life written at the same time. It would not be hard to find out whether the prices quoted were typical of 1895.

A West Country cottage from an illustration in The English Illustrated Magazine, *1889*

EXERCISES AND ACTIVITIES

The following extract is taken from an account of the Peterloo Massacre in 1819. It was written by Samuel Bamford, a Lancashire cotton weaver who was a reformer, a radical, and a political agitator at that time. He wrote the book from which this extract is taken in 1839–42.

Bamford estimated that about 80 000 people assembled at St Peter's Field in Manchester on Monday, 16 August 1819. Most were workers in the local textile industries. Their purpose was to demonstrate in favour of Parliamentary Reform. At that time only a small handful of people, most of them wealthy, were able to vote at elections. Manchester, a large industrial city, was not even represented in Parliament. The organisers of the demonstration, such as Samuel Bamford, wanted the demonstration to be peaceful and law-abiding in order to impress the authorities. He said, 'I hoped their conduct would be marked by a steadiness and seriousness befitting the occasion.'

The meeting was addressed by a fiery Radical speaker called Henry 'Orator' Hunt. Soon after he began to speak, Bamford, who was on the edge of the crowd, heard 'a noise and strange murmur'. Standing on tiptoe, he saw the cavalry 'come trotting sword in hand, round the corner'.

> On the cavalry drawing up they were received with a shout, of good will, as I understood it. They shouted again, waving their sabres over their heads; and then, slackening rein, and striking spur into their steeds, they dashed forward, and began cutting the people.
> 'Stand fast,' I said, 'they are riding upon us, stand fast.' And there was a general cry in our quarter of 'Stand fast.' The cavalry were in confusion: they evidently could not, with all the weight of man and horse, penetrate that compact mass of human beings; and their sabres were plied to hew a way through naked held-up hands, and defenceless heads; and then chopped limbs, and wound-gaping skulls were seen; and groans and cries were mingled with the din of that horrid confusion. 'Ah! ah!' 'for shame! for shame!' was shouted. Then, 'Break! break! they are killing them in front, and they cannot get away'; and there was a general cry of 'break! break!' For a moment the crowd held back as in a pause; then was a rush, heavy and resistless as a headlong sea; and a sound like low thunder, with screams, prayers, and imprecations from the crowd-moiled, and sabre-doomed, who could not escape.
>
> Samuel Bamford, *Passages in the Life of a Radical*,
> written between 1839 and 1842, and first published in 1844

1 *If 'turmoil' means 'confusion' what do you think 'crowd-moiled' means? What did Bamford mean by 'sabre-doomed'?*

2 *Go through the extract using the checklists for historical evidence on page 9 and for eyewitness evidence on page 41.*

3   Is it likely that anyone caught up in the crowd on that day would ever forget it? What importance should be given to the fact that Bamford wrote his account in 1839–42, not 1819?

4   Compare Bamford's account of the Peterloo Massacre with other eyewitness accounts, for instance those printed on pages 237–40 of Philip Sauvain, British Economic and Social History: 1700–1870 (Stanley Thornes, 1987).

Who were the 'Manchester Heroes' in this cartoon?

Different Types of Historical Evidence

RELICS FROM THE PAST

Some of the relics from the past which we can see and touch are called *archaeological remains*. Archaeology is the science which studies the past through the materials left behind by people in the past. Much of what we know from archaeology has been discovered by unearthing pottery, tools, bones, and the remains of buildings buried in the ground. Thirty years ago people thought of archaeology as being concerned only with prehistory – the period before there were written documents to tell us about past events and past peoples. This has changed. Nowadays archaeologists study the recent past as well as the distant past. Industrial archaeology in particular, is concerned with the tools, machines, engines, mills and early factories which marked the beginnings of the Industrial and Agricultural Revolutions.

Checklist — Relics from the Past

Studying relics from the past at a site such as an old mill, or in a museum, or from photographs, can be a very useful way of backing up what you know about social and economic history from other historical sources, like documents. If you do make such a study, this checklist may be useful in helping you to find out more about the subject.

1 *What was the purpose of the tool, machine, vehicle or building you are studying? What was it used for? Why was it built or made?*

2 *Can you date the object or building either exactly or approximately?*

3 *Where is it situated now or where was it found? Where did it come from originally?*

4 *What does it tell us about people in the past?*

Going through the Checklist

Back-to-back houses in Teesside

SOURCE A

1   *What was the purpose of the tool, machine, vehicle or building you are studying? What was it used for? Why was it built or made?*

These are cheap back-to-back terraced houses which were probably built for the workers in a shipyard or factory nearby. One row of terraced houses was built facing one way with another row of houses built against the rear wall, back-to-back, facing in the opposite direction. In this way the houses inside the row shared their side walls with their neighbours on either side and their back walls with their neighbours in the houses in the next street. This made the houses much cheaper to build. In a sense they were rather like two-storey blocks of flats.

2   *Can you date the object or building either exactly or approximately?*

Yes – approximately. The style of building is typical of the terraced houses built in the second half of the nineteenth century. So the houses were probably built between 1850 and 1900.

3   *Where is it situated now or where was it found? Where did it come from originally?*

The buildings were photographed in Middlesbrough in Teesside in about 1980. A photograph like this has value as a record of buildings which have since been demolished or renovated.

4 *What does it tell us about people in the past?*

It helps to explain why Victorian housing aided the spread of diseases, such as tuberculosis, cholera and typhoid. Very large families had to live in these small, gloomy houses (only one wall had windows). Sanitary conditions were often primitive. Overcrowding obviously helped to spread infectious diseases (often by droplets when coughing) and contagious diseases (by direct contact).

Doorway of The Hansom Cab public house in Earls Court Road, London

SOURCE B

1 *What was the purpose of the tool, machine, vehicle or building you are studying? What was it used for? Why was it built or made?*

The modern photograph shows a carriage lamp and the hood from a two-wheeled hansom cab mounted above the entrance to a modern public house. The lamp had a wick and used oil as fuel. It provided enough light to enable the carriage to be seen by other vehicles and threw a faint light on to the road to enable the driver of the carriage (travelling at no more than the speed of a slow bicycle) to see his way forward. The hood provided protection for the passenger or passengers (maximum two) – as you can see in the 1910 photograph.

2 *Can you date the object or building either exactly or approximately?*

Yes – approximately. The first hansom cabs were introduced into Britain in 1825 and were swiftly replaced by motor cabs in about 1910. Since this public house commemorates the hansom cab we can guess that it probably dates from 1910 or thereafter and that the hood and the carriage lamps were taken from one of the last hansom cabs still in service at that time.

3 *Where is it situated now or where was it found? Where did it come from originally?*

It forms part of the entrance to The Hansom Cab public house in Earls Court Road, London. It almost certainly came originally from a London hansom cab.

4 *What does it tell us about people in the past?*

It shows clearly the link between the first motor cars – the horseless carriage of the 1890s – and the horse-drawn carriages which preceded them. Even today some modern sports cars have folding hoods (like the one on the hansom cab) and car headlamps are similar to the old carriage lamps.

Hansom cab in 1910

EXERCISES AND ACTIVITIES

Look at the relics from the past shown in the photographs below. Go through the checklist with each one and see what you can deduce from the photographs. Are there relics like these in your town?

Gas lamp in London's West End

Boot scrapers outside the door of a Georgian house in Saffron Walden in Essex

DOCUMENTARY EVIDENCE

Anything that is written down (such as a letter), or printed (such as a newspaper) is called *documentary evidence*. It includes wills, Acts of Parliament, advertisements, posters, timetables, receipts, letters, journals, diaries, and anything else in written or printed form. For instance, this Post Office poster, printed in London in 1840, is an example of documentary evidence.

POST OFFICE REGULATIONS.

On and after the 10th January, a Letter not exceeding **half an ounce in weight,** may be sent from any part of the United Kingdom, to any other part, for **One Penny,** if paid when posted, or for **Twopence** if paid when delivered.

THE SCALE OF RATES,

If paid when posted, is as follows, for all Letters, whether sent by the General or by any Local Post,

Not exceeding ½ Ounce .... **One Penny.**
Exceeding ½ Ounce, but not exceeding 1 Ounce   **Twopence.**
Ditto   1 Ounce............... 2 Ounces **Fourpence.**
Ditto   2 Ounces .... 3 Ounces **Sixpence.**
and so on; an additional Two-pence for every additional Ounce. With but few exceptions, the WEIGHT is limited to Sixteen Ounces.

If not paid when posted, double the above Rates are charged on Inland Letters.

COLONIAL LETTERS.

If sent by Packet Twelve Times, if by Private Ship Eight Times, the above Rates.

FOREIGN LETTERS.

The Packet Rates which vary, will be seen at the Post Office   The Ship Rates are the same as the Ship Rates for Colonial Letters,

As regards Foreign and Colonial Letters, there is no limitation as to weight. All sent outwards, with a few exceptions, which may be learnt at the Post Office, must be paid when posted as heretofore.

Letters intended to go by Private Ship must be marked *"Ship Letter"*

Some arrangements of minor importance, which are omitted in this Notice, may be seen in that placarded at the Post Office.

No Articles should be transmitted by Post, which are liable to *injury* by being stamped, or by being crushed in the Bags.

It is particularly requested that all Letters may be *fully* and *legibly* addressed, and *posted as early* as convenient.

January 7th, 1840.

By Authority :—J Hartnell, London.

Post Office poster 1840. To which important event does it refer?

The first thing you need to do when you see evidence like this is to read it through carefully to make sure you understand what it means. Then examine it closely to see how far you can trust it as a reliable piece of historical evidence. In this particular case, this would be unnecessary. There is no reason to doubt an official notice of this type.

The master checklist opposite combines the earlier checklists printed on pages 9 (historical evidence), 20 (facts and opinions), 24 (accuracy and reliability), 28 (bias and prejudice), 35 (gaps and contradictions), and 41 (eyewitnesses and hearsay evidence). It is also printed at the back of the book on page 129 as a convenient point of reference. When you use this master checklist, use only the checkpoints which are relevant to the extract you are studying, or for which you have sufficient information to make a sensible response.

Master Checklist — **Documentary Evidence**

1 What does the source tell you about the past?

2 What is the origin of the source? What type of evidence is it (e.g. diary, letter, newspaper report)? Is it likely to be reliable?

3 Why was the source written? Was it written to justify the writer's actions? Does the writer try to take credit for successes which other people claim for themselves? Does the writer put the blame for failures on to other people?

4 When was the source written? Is it a primary source, dating from the time of the event which it describes? Or is it a secondary source?

5 Is there any clue or statement to show that it is an actual eyewitness account? Was the writer in a good position to say what happened? Does the source agree with other eyewitness accounts of the same event? Are there any reasons for thinking the eyewitness cannot be trusted entirely?

6 If the source was written years after the event, is there any reason to doubt the accuracy of the writer's memory?

7 Which parts of the extract seem to you to be opinions, and not facts which can be proved right or wrong? Are the opinions based on facts or on prejudice? Has the writer used words of approval or disapproval, or colourful or exaggerated phrases, to try to influence the reader?

8 Does the author show any other signs of bias or prejudice? Does the writer appear to take sides in an argument?

9 Are there any obvious mistakes or errors of fact in the extract? Which statements are supported by facts you know about from other sources? Does anything in the extract contradict other sources, or facts which you already know to be true?

10 Does the account give a distorted view of events which actually occurred? Has the author left out facts which tell a different story? Is any part of the extract an obvious lie or exaggeration? Are there any obvious gaps in the evidence, such as missing dates, facts, or personalities?

Going through the Checklist

Here is an example of the way in which the master checklist can be used to evaluate a historical source.

Advertisement in Trewman's Exeter Flying-Post, Thursday, 6 August 1829

Cullompton Turnpike.

NOTICE is hereby given, That the TOLLS arising at the TOLL GATES and STOP GATE upon the CULLOMPTON TURNPIKE ROAD, at BEER, in the parish of Broadclist, and at the STOP GATE near thereto, called or known by the several names of *Beer Gate* and *Stop Gate*, will be LET BY AUCTION, to the Best Bidder, at the HALF-MOON INN, in Cullompton, on THURSDAY, the *Twenty-Seventh Day of August next*, between the hours of Twelve and Two, in the manner directed by the Act passed in the Third Year of his Majesty George the Fourth, "For Regulating Turnpike Roads,"—which Tolls produced the last Year the Sum of £487. above the Expences of collecting them, and will be put up at that Sum.—Whoever happens to be the Best Bidder, must, at the same time, pay One Month in advance (if required) of the Rent at which such Tolls may be let, and give Security, with sufficient Sureties, to the satisfaction of the Trustees of the said Turnpike Road, for Payment of the rest of the Money monthly.

FRED. LEIGH,
Clerk to the Trustees of the said Turnpike Road.
Dated 28th July, 1829.   [1319

---

1   *What does the source tell you about the past?*

It tells us that the right to collect tolls on a turnpike was let to the highest bidder at a public auction. It also tells us that in 1828 these tolls brought in an income of nearly £500 – a substantial sum of money at that time.

2   *What is the origin of the source? What type of evidence is it (e.g. diary, letter, newspaper report)? Is it likely to be reliable?*

It is obviously an authentic advertisement printed in a local newspaper – *Trewman's Exeter Flying-Post.*

3   *Why was the source written? Was it written to justify the writer's actions? Does the writer try to take credit for successes which other people claim for themselves? Does the writer put the blame for failures on to other people?*

The notice was printed in a local newspaper in order to attract likely bidders to the auction.

4 *When was the source written? Is it a primary source dating from the time of the event which it describes? Or is it a secondary source?*

It is a primary source since it comes from an issue of the newspaper printed three weeks before the day of the auction.

Checkpoints 5–10 do not apply since this is an authentic notice stating matters of fact not opinion.

EXERCISES AND ACTIVITIES

Read the following extracts and then for each one go through the master checklist on page 53. What does Source A tell you about policing in London in the early eighteenth century? What do Sources B, C, D and E tell you about the miners' strike in 1984–5?

SOURCE A

THE WATCH

LONDON, December 16, 1725

London does not possess any watchmen, either on foot or on horseback as in Paris, to prevent murder and robbery; the only watchman you see is a man in every street carrying a stick and a lantern, who, every time the clock strikes, calls out the hour and state of the weather. The first time this man goes on his rounds he pushes the doors of the shops and houses with his stick to ascertain whether they are properly fastened, and if they are not he warns the proprietors.

A Foreign View of England – The Letters of Monsieur Cesar de Saussure To His Family, translated and edited by Madame Van Muyden, John Murray, 1902

SOURCE B

After 12 months Scargill's army calls off the strike

SURRENDER

● NO agreement on closing pits
● NO amnesty for serious crime

Daily Mail, *Monday, 4 March 1985*

SOURCE C

The Sun, Monday,
4 March 1985

'Traitor' taunt as Scargill caves in

By TOM CONDON and
TONY MAGUIRE

THE marathon pit strike ended yesterday in bitter defeat for Arthur Scargill.

Shouts of "traitor" and "sell-out" echoed around the miners' leader as he announced a return to work tomorrow.

Some pitmen crowding round him seemed to spit at him.

DECISION

Mr Scargill was finally forced to give in by his own members —WITHOUT a deal on pit closures and WITHOUT an amnesty for the 700 men sacked during the year-long dispute.

Surrender came on a tight 98-91 vote by an NUM delegate conference at the TUC headquarters in London.

SOURCE D

The Guardian, Monday,
4 March 1985

One of the most significant chapters in Britain's trade union history was closed last night when the miners reluctantly agreed to call off their strike in a mood of bitterness and tears, almost a year after it had begun.

A delegate conference of the National Union of Mineworkers at TUC headquarters in London decided by 98 votes to 91 to abandon the strike without an agreement with the National Coal Board and call for an organised return to work tomorrow.

To the end, Mr Arthur Scargill, the NUM president, spat defiance at the NCB, the Government, the TUC and the media, maintaining that while the strike was at an end, the struggle would go on.

The tactics of the union will be to fight pit closures at local level and to cause as much inconvenience as possible to the NCB in the process. By returning to work without an agreement, the union has still not resolved its problems with the NCB over pay.

LOSERS ALL

Strike over —now for reckoning

"We've won Nigel, we've won"

THERE is only one certainty about the ending of the miners' strike, the longest major industrial conflict in our history—everyone is a loser.

It is an end without any clear solution. An end that will drag its aftermath into the next months, possibly years. The legend will long outlive even the bitterness.

At the centre of it all has been miners' president Arthur Scargill. A remarkable figure, whatever you may think.

Yesterday was possibly the worst moment of his life when he was forced, with angry reluctance, to acknowledge the end and then to announce it to a media he despises.

Left to him, there would have been no final acceptance of the inevitable.

And even when it was all over, by that memorable 98-91 vote, he still insisted: "This union will fight on to retain pits, jobs and communities."

Emotions

It was like some echo from a deserted canyon.

Tough men wept when the news filtered down.

Now comes the reckoning of bills, wounds, mortgage payments, raw emotions, coal faces that will never re-open, "scab" signs chalked across walls and homes . . . and a thousand other elements.

The cost to the nation? Who can tell. The Government reckons about £2 billion.

By GEOFFREY GOODMAN
Mirror Group Industrial Editor

SOURCE E

Daily Mirror, Monday, 4
March 1985

NEWSPAPERS AND MAGAZINES

Newspapers have been published in Britain for over 300 years. They were first taxed in 1712 and this made newspapers costly to buy. In 1797, the government raised the newspaper tax, called Stamp Duty, in order to make it too expensive for ordinary people to buy a newspaper. They did not want newspapers putting revolutionary ideas about freedom, justice, and fair play into the heads of the masses. When Stamp Duty was abolished in 1855 it paved the way for cheap newspapers. It was not until the end of the century, however, that the first really cheap newspapers were published for the millions of people who could now read – thanks to the improvements in state education in the late nineteenth century.

The first of the popular newspapers, the *Daily Mail*, cost a halfpenny (about 0.2p) when it was first published in 1896. Since then many other popular cheap newspapers have been published as well, including the *Daily Express* (1900), *Daily Mirror* (1904), and *The Sun* (1969). The first illustrated weekly magazines were begun in the 1840s with the founding of *The Illustrated London News* and the humorous weekly *Punch*. Many of these magazines and newspapers relied on advertisements so that they could be sold cheaply. Old newspapers and magazines are an invaluable source of historical evidence. Some, such as *The Times*, have been copied on to microfilm.

The great advantage of newspapers and magazines as historical sources is that they were written at the time as contemporary news reports. So they are primary historical sources. They were also written for ordinary people to read, so they are often more interesting and easier to read than official documents. This is not to say that they are always to be trusted. Far from it. Many news reports were based on hearsay evidence, on biased reports from prejudiced journalists, or even taken straight from the columns of other newspapers. There is often no way of knowing what has been left out of a report or how reliable the anonymous writer was. Opinions are sometimes quoted as if they were facts. Many newspapers were (and still are) biased in favour of a particular political party. Popular newspapers often distort or colour the facts in order to make a news story more interesting to their readers.

EXERCISES AND ACTIVITIES

Look at the cuttings on page 58 from three newspapers printed during the General Strike in May 1926.

A food convoy during the General Strike

SOURCE A

Daily Mail, *Wednesday, 5 May 1926*

Yesterday the general strike came into force, showing that there is no extremity of violence from which the persons behind this conspiracy will shrink. Their ostensible leaders, the Parliamentary politicians – whose business it is to act the role of decoy ducks and win the support of the muddle-headed and simple – may deal in sobstuff about the "terrible situation", and their reluctance to go to extremes. But while they talk, their followers act. While the House of Commons is treated to lacrimose speeches, the country is being "held up".

The British nation is eager to support its Government. It is waiting for its Government to act. It is looking to its Government to act. It is capable of any effort and of any sacrifice. But a nation cannot rally unless there is action; it cannot feel enthusiasm for a policy of sitting still. It never admired the policy of Kerensky, whose fault it was to imagine that words were the equivalent of deeds. When a fight is in progress (and the leaders of this strike have not hesitated to use the word "war") the only thing to do is to win it, not to think of what will happen if we do not win it. That is the policy which caused the failure of Jutland.

SOURCE B

The British Worker, *Monday, 10 May 1926*

NATION BEHIND THE T.U.C.

What a London Park Meeting Revealed

£55 COLLECTION

The quiet determination of the men on strike has impressed the outside public. The strikers' confidence and enthusiasm are contagious. They have spread to other sections of the nation.

"They don't look a bit like unemployed," remarked a young woman onlooker, who stood on the step of a West Norwood villa while a procession of transport strikers, be-medalled and in Sunday attire, marched in fours to Brockwell Park.

The immense crowd in the park gave a clear indication of where the sympathies of the British nation lie in this dispute. Many of the crowd were trade unionists, including strikers and their families, but at least a third of them were of the class which the Premier loves to call "the general public," bank and insurance clerks, small shopkeepers, holders of season tickets, dwellers in suburban villas.

THE END OF THE GENERAL STRIKE.

QUESTIONS OF PRAISE AND BLAME.

Everybody's first thought to-day must be one of profound satisfaction that the general strike is over. The British people have come with credit out of a severe ordeal. During an unprecedented struggle, extending over nine days, not a cartridge—not even a blank cartridge—has been fired by a soldier, and no single fatal collision has occurred between the strikers and the civil power. There has been no food shortage, no panic, and wonderfully little loss of temper on either side. In a fair trial of strength, which we hope may never be repeated, the nation has stood up to the general strike and overcome it.

Trade unionists, we believe, will agree that the calling of the general strike was a serious blunder. It placed their movement in a false position. Mr. Lloyd George, in a message sent out early yesterday before the settlement, stated the matter in two sentences. "If," he said,

"The trade unions inflict a defeat on the Government, it will be an encouragement to the extreme elements in Labour to resort in future to the general strike as a weapon of offence, whenever they find their purpose thwarted by the normal working of democratic institutions. Such a defeat would sooner or later end the experiment of popular government in these islands."

The time will come later to review the situation fully, and to decide the respective responsibilities of the Government and the T.U.C., but some things are clear already. The Government committed a disastrous blunder, when on the night of Sunday, May 2, after its basis for continuing to treat with its miners had been actually accepted by the T.U.C., it abruptly banged the door on negotiations. But for that, it seems certain that a settlement would have been reached without a strike. There was nothing unusual in it being deferred to the final 24 hours; settlements very often are. What was unusual, was that, by the Government's folly, the final 24 hours were suddenly made unavailable for negotiation. Mr. Baldwin has never been a cheap Prime Minister, but this was one of his costliest mistakes.

SOURCE C

The Daily Chronicle, *Thursday, 13 May 1926*

1   Go through each of these sources with the aid of the master checklist on page 53.

2   Which of these newspapers show political bias, and in which direction? How do they try to convince their readers?

3   Compare the different ways in which all three newspapers appear to suggest that they know what the attitude of the general public was to the strike.

4   Which newspaper would you have chosen to read had you wanted an unbiased account of the General Strike?

JOURNALS, DIARIES AND LETTERS

This is a page from the holiday diary of a Lancashire teacher on holiday in Plymouth in 1923. Why do you think he wanted to go to the 'old camp'? What sort of 'Pictures' were 'Very Good'? How did he travel to Stoke Beach?

Monday. 30th
Went to town for a film & in the morning & walked to the old camp in the afternoon with baby. Rained - first time I used my umbrella since coming. Pictures — Very Good Pleasant Evening.

Tuesday 31·7·23
Chara to Stoke Beach. Beautiful ride through Country Lanes Lunch on arrival. Then climbed on rocks & waded in sea. Photos Snapped in various positions. Sheltered from short shower in a cavern. Visited Revelstoke Churchyard and looked at remains of Church. Tea at Verandah

Travel journals, diaries, and letters are an important source of historical evidence. This is because they are primary sources. The descriptions are usually eyewitness accounts, and the writers often recall conversations which were still fresh in the mind when they wrote them. The more interesting personal diaries and journals have been published; the most famous is probably the *Diary of Samuel Pepys* written in the 1660s.

The diary entries you will see will probably fall into two main groups. The first group contains the many diaries which have been published primarily because the diarist is or was someone famous (such as Gladstone) or close to someone famous (such as Frances Stevenson, secretary to Lloyd George – see pages 17–19).

The second group contains diaries which have been published because they throw unusual or fascinating light on the past through the eyes of ordinary people with no particular claim to fame. These diaries are almost always interesting and provide a valuable source of information about everyday life in the past. For instance, The Reverend James Woodforde, the rector of a small Norfolk village near Norwich, wrote a well-known diary in the late eighteenth and early nineteenth centuries. His diary tells us about the perils and discomforts of a journey by stage coach. It also tells us about taxes, smugglers, entertainments, servants, illnesses, food, farming, and many other topics of interest in social and economic history.

Collections of letters written by famous people, such as Queen Victoria, have also been published. These are particularly useful where the replies are published as well. Letters between politicians often help historians to discover the reasons why actions were taken in the past.

Travel journals (even your holiday diary!) are also of value. One of the most useful sources of information about farming, industry, towns and transport in the early eighteenth century is the travel journal which was written by Daniel Defoe after travelling through many parts of Britain in about 1720.

You can also find articles written by journalists in newspapers and magazines under headings such as 'London Day By Day' or 'Notes of the Week'. There are also printed journals of events, often published under titles such as *Annals of Yorkshire* or *Annals of Our Time*. These Annals are not necessarily primary historical sources, since they may have been written many years after the events they describe.

At first glance journals, diaries and letters seem to be an ideal historical source. Those by famous people are often especially interesting where they tell us why certain actions were taken, and what the writer thought as well as what he or she did. But there are a number of drawbacks. Famous people know that their letters and diaries will probably be published for everyone to read. This why they are often written as if the writer is attempting to justify or excuse certain actions. It is difficult to be certain that the writer is being honest. The diaries of ordinary people are often more revealing. Samuel Pepys tells us far more in his diary than he told people to their faces.

EXERCISES AND ACTIVITIES

The following sources all relate to a serious problem which affected London in the middle of the nineteenth century. You can see how this subject was treated in different ways in Sources A to F.

The first source comes from the published diary of a Norfolk clergyman, the Reverend Benjamin Armstrong, vicar of East Dereham from 1850 to 1888.

SOURCE A

Took the children by boat from Vauxhall Bridge to show them the great buildings. The ride on the water was refreshing except for the stench. What a pity that this noble river should be made a common sewer.

10 July 1855

The second source is a cartoon which was published in the humorous magazine *Punch* about a week after Armstrong's trip on the river. Professor Michael Faraday was a very famous scientist.

SOURCE B

FARADAY GIVING HIS CARD TO FATHER THAMES; AND WE HOPE THE DIRTY FELLOW WILL CONSULT THE LEARNED PROFESSOR.

Cartoon from Punch, *21 July 1855*

The third source is an extract from a regular journal, commenting on current events, which was written each week by an anonymous journalist for a popular weekly picture magazine.

SOURCE C

NOTES OF THE WEEK

26 June 1858

Our representatives have been heroically sitting, both night and morning, to be poisoned by the stenches from the River Thames, whose fatal influence may now be clearly traced in the Registrar-General's Report of the past week. About one hundred deaths in excess of those for which we have a right to look in London during the middle week of June are recorded. Two children have died of cholera, and one strong man, who on his death-bed deliberately attributed his fate to the poisonous fumes from the water.

The Illustrated London News, 26 June 1858

The fourth source is an extract from a day-by-day journal of the important events which occurred in Britain between 1837 and 1868.

SOURCE D

30 June 1858

The state of the Thames during this month gave rise to much anxious deliberation. Parliamentary Committees could not sit in the rooms overlooking the river; several of the officers were laid up by sickness; the attendance of members was as brief as possible ... In the Courts at Westminster, judges and juries performed their duties under a sense of danger, and got away as quickly as possible ... The month throughout was the hottest on record ...

Joseph Irving, *Annals of Our Time*, 1869

The fifth source comes from a collection of the published letters of the well-known Victorian novelist, Charles Dickens.

SOURCE E

Gad's Hill, Wednesday, Seventh July, 1858

My Dear Cerjat

... You will have read in the papers that the Thames in London is most horrible. I have to cross Waterloo or London Bridge to get to the railroad when I come down here, and I can certify that the offensive smells, even in that short whiff, have been of a most head-and-stomach distending nature. Nobody knows what is to be done; at least everybody knows a plan, and everybody else knows it won't do; in the meantime cartloads of chloride of lime are shot into the filthy stream, and do something I hope ...

Charles Dickens

The sixth source is a cartoon which appeared in *Punch* about three weeks after Dickens wrote his letter.

SOURCE F

HOW DIRTY OLD FATHER THAMES WAS WHITE WASHED.

Punch cartoon, 31 July
1858

1 *Go through the master checklist on page 53 for each written source in turn (i.e. Sources A, C, D, E).*

2 *What do the six sources each tell you about the state of the Thames in London in the 1850s?*

3 *How do the cartoons confirm what you have read in the diary, the letter and the journals?*

4 *Why do you think Professor Faraday is shown 'giving his card to Father Thames'?*

5 *How had the authorities tried to cure the problem?*

6 *What do you think was the cause of the problem?*

7 *What do the first two sources (dated 1855) have in common with the last four sources (dated 1858)?*

8 *Why were people so concerned about the stench from the Thames? What does this tell you about their understanding of the spread of diseases?*

Read this account of a coach journey by a French traveller who went from Northampton to Leicester in about 1782.

This ride from Northampton to Leicester I shall remember as long as I live. The coach drove from the yard through a part of the house. The inside passengers got in in the yard, but we outside were obliged to clamber up on the public street, because we should have had no room for our heads to pass under the gateway.

I was obliged to sit just at the corner of the coach, with nothing to hold by but a sort of little handle fastened at the side. The machine now rolled along with prodigious rapidity over the stones through the town, and every moment we seemed to fly into the air, so that it was almost a miracle that we still stuck to the coach and did not fall. At last, being continually in fear of my life, I crept from the top of the coach, and got snug into the basket among the trunks and packages; but when we came to go downhill then all the trunks and packages began, as it were, to dance around me. I was obliged to suffer this torture nearly an hour, till we came to another hill, when, quite shaken to pieces and badly bruised, I again crept to the top of the coach and took my former seat.

From Harborough to Leicester I had a most dreadful journey, it rained incessantly; and as before we had been covered with dust, we now were soaked with rain.

C.P. Moritz, 1782

9 *Go through the master checklist on page 53. What does this source tell you about stage coaches in the late eighteenth century?*

10 *Why do you think the journal of a foreigner travelling in Britain, such as that of C.P. Moritz, should be particularly interesting and valuable as a source of information about British social and economic history?*

11 *The traveller describes 'a most dreadful journey'. What is the danger of relying on this source as a description of what it was like to travel in a stage coach in 1782?*

MEMOIRS AND ORAL HISTORY

Oral history is spoken history. It is recollections about the past which are told to a historian rather than written down as memoirs. Oral history is usually first recorded on cassette, tape or video, but may be written down at a later date. Oral historians record the reminiscences of ordinary people rather than those of the famous. They include the former coal miner talking about the General Strike in 1926 and the suffragette describing life in prison. Everyone has listened to oral history like this, even if it is only a grandparent talking about the 1930s or parents describing their own schooldays.

Nowadays historians recognise that oral history can make a big contribution to our understanding of the past. It is also a method of writing history which is open to anyone who has a cassette recorder.

Memoirs, on the other hand, are usually written by people of importance, such as a former prime minister or an admiral. The main difference compared with oral history is that they are written down instead of being spoken. They are almost always backed up in detail by documentary evidence, such as diaries, letters, and official documents.

Both types of recollection – the spoken history and the written memoir – may be inaccurate and unreliable historical sources. This is because they depend heavily on human memory, which may or may not be faulty. Older people often tend to remember the past as being either much better or much worse than the present. Only rarely do they seem to think of it as being the same! If people were poor, they were much poorer than today. If they were happy, they were much happier than today! Not surprisingly, people recalling past events tend to justify their own actions. Writers of memoirs may skip over their mistakes and omit the less successful, or more shameful, periods of their lives. Above all, beware of the razor-sharp recollection of events which happened fifty or sixty years ago. This is not eyewitness evidence you can always trust.

EXERCISES AND ACTIVITIES

Use a cassette recorder to make an oral history which you can use when you study a topic in economic and social history, such as agriculture, industry, transport, health, or education. Choose a theme which your older relatives can talk about, like factory working conditions, evacuation during the Second World War, the miners' strike of 1984–5, or recollections of the early days of television, radio, or even the motor car. When you have made the tape recording, treat it as documentary evidence and use the master checklist on page 53 to test the reliability of your historical sources.

USING PROPAGANDA AND ADVERTS

Propaganda is anything which deliberately sets out to persuade you to accept only one particular viewpoint, attitude, or set of facts, irrespective of the truth. At its worst, it is a campaign by ruthless people, such as the Nazis, to distort the truth in order to win backing for a war or a campaign of persecution. At its best, it is an effective advertisement designed to persuade people to give up a habit, such as cigarette smoking, which experts believe could damage their health.

Hoarding at the corner of a street in Victorian London, The Illustrated Sporting and Dramatic News, *1890. How many of these names can you still recognise?*

Propaganda and advertisements can be useful historical sources in social and economic history. Election posters tell us how political parties tried to discredit the policies of their opponents on subjects such as taxation or free trade. Advertisements help us to picture everyday life and to see how shopkeepers tried to sell their goods in the past. They show us the patent medicines and cures which were advertised by quacks at a time when there was little restriction on their activities. Through these advertisements we can get some idea of Victorian attitudes to ill health.

Look at this whisky advertisement which was published in The Sphere on 17 October 1908. What was the aim of the advert? What does it tell you about the early days of motoring? Why would a modern advertiser be most unlikely to produce an advertisement like this in Britain today?

EXERCISES AND ACTIVITIES

1   *Look at the advertisements printed here. What do they tell you about the social and economic history of the Victorian period from 1884 to 1897? What is their value as historical evidence today?*

2   *Which of these advertisements would a newspaper not print today? Why not?*

3   *Which of these products is still advertised today? Compare these adverts with their modern equivalents – whether on television or in print. What changes have taken place (if any) in the way in which goods are advertised? What were the aims of these Victorian advertisers? How did they try to persuade people to buy their products?*

Advertisement for Cadbury's cocoa, The Illustrated Sporting and Dramatic News, 21 June 1884

Advertisement for Fry's cocoa, The Graphic, 26 June 1897

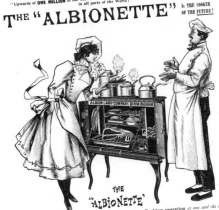

Advertisement for the Albionette cooker, The Graphic, 26 June 1897

Advertisement for Singer's sewing machine, The Sketch, 19 August 1896

Advertisement for Hudson's soap, The Illustrated London News, Christmas 1889

Advertisement for Sunlight soap, The Illustrated London News, 1890

The political posters you can see below were used by the Liberal party before the 1906 General Election to attack the policies of the Conservative party led by A.J. (Arthur) Balfour, the prime minister, and the Tariff Reform League led by Joseph Chamberlain. Chamberlain (who always wore a monocle) was a former minister who had resigned from the government. The Tariff Reform League wanted to protect British farmers and manufacturers against the threat to their livelihoods from cheap foreign imports, such as corn and meat. At that time Britain had a policy of free trade. This meant that foreign producers did not have to pay customs duties on the goods they exported to Britain.

4 *How did the Liberals attempt to persuade electors that Tariff Reform would be bad for their pockets? What did they think of Conservative promises in the past?*

Poster: 'Will it Burst Too?', reproduced in The Illustrated London News, 6 January 1906

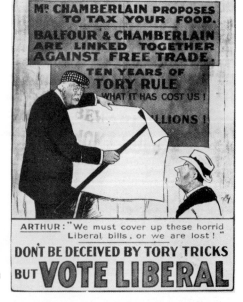

Poster: 'Obscuring the Issue', reproduced in The Illustrated London News, 6 January 1906

EVIDENCE FROM FICTION

Fiction simply means anything which has been invented or made up. Fiction can take many different forms. It includes stories, plays, novels, poems, ballads, rhymes, and the words to songs.

Fiction is often based on fact. Authors in the past, as now, often based their writings on things they had seen themselves in real life. There was little point in trying to get readers involved in the plot of a story if the descriptions of houses, shops, working conditions, schools, and clothes of the characters did not ring true as well. The stories were fictional, but the way of life described was often typical of its time. This can be confirmed by comparing written accounts in novels and stories with factual descriptions, photographs and pictures.

Fiction also throws light on the way in which people behaved, such as their manners and their customs. It can help us to understand how people spoke and their attitudes to servants or to employers. Descriptions of everyday life are often particularly vivid because they are written by excellent writers who knew how to make a scene come to life. This is why fiction is a particularly useful source of historical evidence for the study of economic and social history.

Like most historical sources, however, there are drawbacks. If a writer, such as Charles Dickens, felt strongly about an injustice he often exaggerated the problem, or based his story on a particularly bad case (such as the schoolmaster Wackford Squeers in *Nicholas Nickleby*). There is a danger that some social evils, such as the workhouse, may appear to be much worse in fiction than they really were in fact.

Going through the Checklist

You can apply the same checks to fiction as you would to a factual historical source. For example, read this extract from the novel *The Expedition of Humphry Clinker* by Tobias Smollett, first published in 1770. The master checklist used is the same as the one printed on page 53.

BATH

Hard by the Pump-room, is a coffee-house for the ladies; but my aunt says, young girls are not admitted, inasmuch as the conversation turns upon politics, scandal, philosophy, and other subjects above our capacity; but we are allowed to accompany them to the booksellers' shops, which are charming places of resort; where we read novels, plays, pamphlets, and news-papers, for so small a subscription as a crown a quarter [about 2p a week]; and in these offices of intelligence (as my brother calls them), all the reports of the day, and all the private transactions of the Bath, are first entered and discussed.

1 *What does the source tell you about the past?*

It tells us something about the daily way of life and the attitudes of the wealthy people who went to take the waters in the fashionable spa town of Bath. This extract, in particular, tells us that booksellers in the eighteenth century performed something of the same function as a public library does today – but for a small fee.

2 *What is the origin of the source? Is it likely to be reliable?*

It is by Tobias Smollett. He was a well-known writer in the eighteenth century, who had visited Bath several times.

3 *Why was the source written?*

As an amusing novel describing the expedition of Humphry Clinker to England and Scotland.

4 *When was the source written? Is it a primary source dating from the time of the event which it describes? Or is it a secondary source?*

It is a primary source since it was written in 1770 and describes Great Britain at that time.

Checkpoints 5 to 10 do not apply.

EXERCISES AND ACTIVITIES

Refuge for the destitute in London, The Illustrated London News, *1843*

Read the three extracts which follow. They come from a novel called *Paved with Gold* which was written by Augustus Mayhew, the brother of a famous writer called Henry Mayhew who conducted a detailed survey of the poor of London in the 1850s. *Paved With Gold* was published in 1858 and August Mayhew wrote in the Preface:

Of one thing I may humbly make a boast – the extreme truthfulness with which this book has been written. The descriptions of boy-life in the streets, the habits and customs of donkey-drivers, the peculiarities of tramp-dom and vagrancy, have all resulted from long and patient inquiries among the individuals themselves ... Indeed some portions of this book ... were originally undertaken by me at the request of my brother, Mr Henry Mayhew ...

AT THE ASYLUM FOR THE HOUSELESS POOR

● *The queue waiting to be admitted*
It is a terrible thing to look down upon that squalid crowd from one of the upper windows. There they stand shivering in the snow, with their thin cobwebby garments hanging in tatters about them. Many are without shirts; with their bare skin showing through the rents and gaps, like the hide of a dog with the mange. Some have their greasy garments tied round their wrists and ankles with string, to prevent the piercing wind from blowing up them. A few are without shoes, and these keep one foot only to the ground, while the bare flesh that has had to tramp through the snow is blue and livid-looking, as half-cooked meat.

● *Gaining admittance*
'And where did you sleep last night?' inquired the clerk.
'At Bethnal-green Union, please sir.'
'And where the night before?' broke in the superintendent.
'Well I was at Whitechapel Union, then sir.'
'And what Union the night before that?'
'I think it were St George's in the East. Oh no, sir, it were Stepney, so it were.'
The superintendent gave a look at the gentlemen, as much as to say, 'You see he has made the round of the workhouses;' and then added to the vagrant, 'I suppose you don't like breaking those four bushels of stones the workhouse people give you of a morning?'
The fellow answered with a leer, and another wriggle in his clothes, 'It ain't exactly the kind of physic as suits my complaint, guv'nor.'
When the vagrant had gone, the superintendent said: 'We are obliged to let in such cases as those, for, if we were to shut our doors because some impose upon us, we should be punishing the honest poor more than the dishonest.'

● *The men's accommodation inside*
The ward itself was a long, bare, whitewashed apartment, with square post-like pillars supporting the flat-beamed roof, and reminding the visitor of a large unoccupied store-room . . . Along the floor were arranged what appeared at first sight to be endless rows of empty orange chests, packed closely side by side, so that the boards were divided off into some two hundred shallow-tanpit-like compartments; and these, the visitors soon learnt, were the berths . . . In each of them lay a black mattress, made of some shiny waterproof material, like tarpauling stuffed with straw. At the head of every bunk, hanging against the wall, was a leather, a big 'basil' covering, that looked more like a wine-cooper's apron than a counterpane. These are used as coverlids because they are not only strong and durable, but they do not retain vermin.

1   What was the 'Union'?

2   How does the writer describe the plight of the poor and needy seeking entrance to the asylum? Is he describing reality, or trying to gain the sympathy of the reader, or is he doing both?

3   Why was the vagrant admitted even though he had done the rounds of the workhouses in that part of London?

4   Why did the vagrant not wish to sleep in the workhouse if he could help it?

5   What do these extracts tell you about the care of the poor in London in the middle of the nineteenth century? Do they prove that it was harsh and unsympathetic?

6   Now go through the master checklist on page 53. Use the information from the author's Preface above to say whether you think this extract from a novel is a reliable historical source or not.

EVIDENCE ON MAPS

Maps and plans are another useful source of historical evidence. The first really accurate maps of Britain were published by the Ordnance Survey in the early 1800s. Maps of a town or district from different periods of time are easy to compare, especially if they have been drawn to scale. Maps like these are primary sources. By comparing maps drawn at different periods of time you can find out when a town began to grow outwards. You can compare the information you obtain from old maps with information from census returns showing when and how the town's population grew.

Checklist — **Maps and Plans**

When you use an old map or plan there are certain checks you should make first before using it as a historical source.

1 *When was the map drawn? What does it show? If it is a special map why was it drawn?*

2 *Is the map accurately drawn? Has it got a scale? If not, work out the scale for yourself. Compare measurements on the old map between three landmarks (e.g. churches) and then compare them with the same measurements on a modern map. In this way you can tell if the map was drawn roughly to scale or not (since the three landmarks will not have moved their position since the date when the old map was drawn).*

3 *What is the particular value of the map (if any) as a source of historical information?*

Going through the Checklist

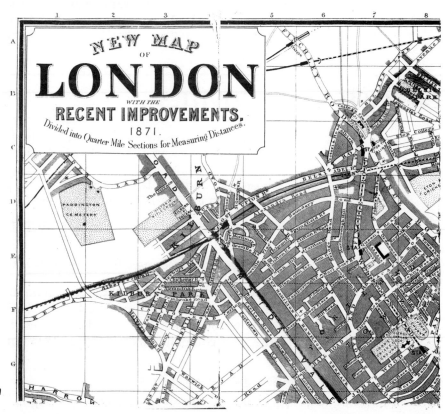

Map of part of London in 1871

Look at the map extract on the previous page.

1   *When was the map drawn? What does it show? If it is a special map why was it drawn?*

This is a general map which was drawn in 1871. It shows the Kilburn Park area of London.

2   *Is the map accurately drawn? Has it got a scale? If not, work out the scale for yourself.*

It is drawn to a scale in which each square has sides a quarter of a mile (400 metres) long, except for the first column. If you work out the map scale from this you will find that it was drawn to a scale of about 1 : 28 500.

3   *What is the particular value of the map (if any) as a source of historical information?*

This map would be a very useful source of information if you were studying the growth of London in the late nineteenth century. As you can see it shows the edge of London's built-up area by 1871. A comparison between this map and a map published ten years later in 1881 would tell you whether this area took part in the rapid growth of London's suburbs in the late nineteenth century. A map like this is also of great use to anyone wanting to find the dates of the buildings in this area. Those built on the open spaces shown on the map must have been built after 1871.

EXERCISES AND ACTIVITIES

Find a copy of a large-scale modern map of London which shows all or part of the Kilburn Park area. A map like this can be found in a road atlas.

1   *Compare measurements taken between the same points on the two maps. Confirm that the 1871 map is accurately drawn to scale.*

2   *What new streets and built-up areas have covered all or part of this area in the last hundred years?*

3   *Which streets and roads have been given new names since 1871? Why?*

Look at the map extract showing the area near Southampton. It must have been drawn at some time between 1834 and 1839. We know this because the map shows the railway line of the London and Southampton Railway Company. This company was founded in 1834 but changed its name in 1839.

4   *Assess the map using the checklist.*

5   *Which features on this map could not be seen on a similar map today?*

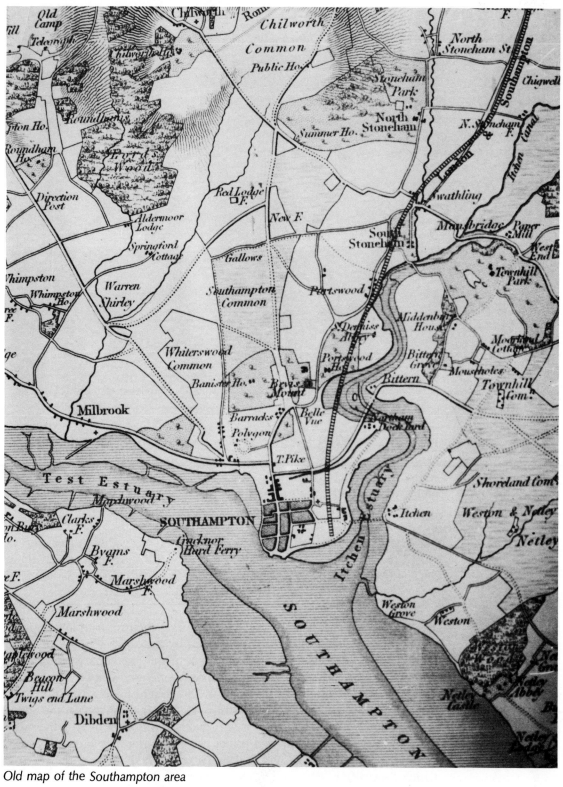

Old map of the Southampton area

FACTS FROM PICTURES

Engraving of a picture by William Hogarth showing a London street scene in about 1740

Pictures of everyday life and pictures created shortly after an event are called *contemporary pictures*. Historians often use them as primary sources. They include paintings, sketches, cartoons, drawings, engravings, pictures on pottery, pictures on stamps, pictures on song sheets, statues, carvings, etc.

Many artists have used their pictures to say something about the society in which they live. The wealth of detail in Hogarth's pictures makes them one of the most important sources of information we have about the social and economic history of Britain in the early eighteenth century.

The main drawback to the use of contemporary pictures is that we cannot always be certain that the picture created by the artist actually portrays real things. The concern of many artists in the past was to produce a pleasing picture which was well composed and well drawn or painted. The artist who painted a cotton mill in 1800 might have wanted to show how impressive or how ugly the mill was, rather than record the scene exactly as he or she saw it. This is why two illustrators depicting the same scene or event can sometimes produce two very different pictures. The two pictures opposite both depict the same event. Make a list of the ways in which they differ.

Launching a new lifeboat at Blackpool, The Illustrated London News, *10 October 1885*

Launching a new lifeboat at Blackpool, The Graphic, *10 October 1885*

Another problem is that we cannot always be certain that the pictures we see were actually drawn or painted on the spot or even that they were based on sketches actually made in the field. Some illustrations were drawn from photographs, or based on newspaper reports and eyewitness accounts. Many detailed and lifelike pictures were 'imagined' by the artist in a studio. As a consequence we cannot always be sure that realistic pictures of people, places and events are the eyewitness primary sources they may at first appear to suggest.

Even a picture accompanying a news item in an illustrated news magazine or newspaper could have been drawn in the studio rather than at the scene of the event. When the first issue of *The Illustrated London News* was published in 1842 it carried a news report and picture of a great fire in Hamburg in Germany. But the artist had not been to Hamburg – instead, he copied an old picture of the city, made flames come out of the buildings, and drew in figures of people to show the crowds!

'View of the Conflagration of Hamburgh', The Illustrated London News, *14 May 1842*

A further drawback is that in many cases you will not be able to find out much about the origins of the contemporary pictures you see. This is partly because many pictures were drawn by anonymous or unknown artists and partly because pictures are often reproduced in books without giving an indication of their actual origin.

Cartoons are another important source of information used by historians studying social and economic history. They often reflect the concern felt by ordinary people for everyday problems, such as slums, pollution, strikes, transport delays, etc. Many cartoons were drawn to make people laugh. But some were drawn to make people react in other ways – to make them angry, or sad, or to try to persuade them to vote in a particular way.

Checklist — **Pictures from the Past**

You can see how each of these checkpoints applies to the pictures on pages 82–6.

1   *Does the picture attempt realistically to portray people, events, buildings, etc., or does it poke fun at them by means of a cartoon or an exaggerated drawing (called a caricature)?*

2   *What does the picture show? What does it tell us about the past?*

3   *When was the picture drawn? Was it drawn at roughly the same time as the event or feature it depicts? Is it a primary source? If no date is given can you estimate roughly the date when it was drawn from the clothes worn by the people in the picture, from styles of vehicle (such as motor cars), or from other clues?*

4   *Why was the picture drawn or painted? Was it simply an illustration (e.g. to accompany a news item or to illustrate a book), or is there any reason to think the artist was using the picture to make you feel in a certain way about the events or people depicted? For instance, was it drawn or painted to make you want to protest against an injustice, or to feel excited, or sad, or nostalgic for an old way of life, or patriotic, or self-satisfied, or envious of someone else's way of life?*

5   *Does the picture show something which could not be shown in any other way, such as the interior of a courtroom where photographs are not permitted?*

6   *Even if it looks like a realistic picture, is there any reason to think it is a product of the artist's imagination rather than a portrayal of an actual scene or event?*

7   *If the picture is a cartoon, what was the artist getting at? What does the cartoon tell you about the topic, events or people portrayed? What does it tell you about the attitude of the artist who drew the cartoon or of the magazine which published it?*

'Battle of A-gin-court'.
This cartoon was
drawn by George
Cruikshank in 1838.
What was the joke?
What do you think was
his reason for drawing
this cartoon?

Look at this picture,
one of a set by William
Hogarth called 'Times
of Day'. This is an
engraving of 'Morning'
and it shows the area
near Covent Garden in
London in about 1730.
Is this a realistic
picture or do you think
Hogarth was poking
fun at these people?
What historical
information does the
picture provide?

'Keen for a Morning Round' appeared in The Graphic on 6 July 1906. Even if we did not know the exact date, we could guess that it dates from the Edwardian period (1901–10) just by looking at the style of the motor vehicle and at the very distinctive motoring bonnets worn by these Edwardian ladies.

Scene on London's embankment showing stockbrokers returning home in the rush hour. See if you can estimate roughly the date when this picture was drawn. What does it tell you about London at that time? Why do you think the artist drew the picture? What did he want you to feel?

Drawing of Christabel Pankhurst in court, The Sphere, *31 October 1908*

This realistic picture of the Manchester Ship Canal appeared in The Illustrated London News *on 3 February 1883, eleven years before the canal was opened! It is an artist's impression of what the canal would look like when completed.*

This cartoon appeared in Punch *on 23 October 1935. It shows that over fifty years ago people were already aware that ribbon development was destroying the countryside.*

CANNOT RIBBON DEVELOPMENT BE DISGUISED?
Work for our Artists and Scene-painters

Going through the Checklist

SOURCE A

Punch *cartoon,*
15 April 1848

"NOT SO VERY UNREASONABLE!!! EH?"

1 *Does the picture attempt realistically to portray people, events, buildings, etc., or does it poke fun at them by means of a cartoon or an exaggerated drawing (called a caricature)?*

It is a cartoon from *Punch*.

2 *What does the picture show? What does it tell us about the past?*

It shows a working man (a Chartist) delivering the Charter to the prime minister in 1848. The Charter was a massive petition containing millions of signatures, most of them from the working class. They were demanding voting rights, e.g. one man, one vote.

3 *When was the picture drawn? Was it drawn at roughly the same time as the event or feature it depicts? Is it a primary source?*

This is a primary source since it was published on 15 April 1848.

4 *Why was the picture drawn or painted?*

It was drawn at the time of a great Chartist meeting in London which the government feared might lead to a serious riot, if not a rebellion. To counter any such danger they put the Duke of Wellington in charge of the police and army in the city.

Checkpoints 5 and 6 do not apply.

7 *If the picture is a cartoon, what was the artist getting at? What does the cartoon tell you about the events or the people portrayed? What does it tell you about the attitude of the artist who drew the cartoon or of the magazine which published it?*

The artist says that the demands of the Chartists were not so very unreasonable and that the fears of the Government were unfounded.

SOURCE B

An engraving of the smoking chimneys of Halifax, The Illustrated London News, *5 August 1882*

1 *Does the picture attempt realistically to portray people, events, buildings, etc., or does it poke fun at them by means of a cartoon or an exaggerated drawing (called a caricature)?*

This is a very realistic drawing with the detail of a photograph. In fact it is highly likely that it was drawn from a photograph in the studio rather than on a hillside overlooking Halifax.

2 *What does the picture show? What does it tell us about the past?*

It shows factory chimneys crowding the narrow valley in which Halifax is situated. It shows that smoke pollution was obviously a major problem in industrial towns over a hundred years ago. It shows us what a woollen textile town looked like in 1882.

3 *When was the picture drawn? Was it drawn at roughly the same time as the event or feature it depicts? Is it a primary source?*

This is a primary source drawn in 1882.

4 *Why was the picture drawn or painted?*

It was drawn to illustrate a news item in *The Illustrated London News.*

6 *Even if it looks like a realistic picture, is there any reason to think it is a product of the artist's imagination rather than a portrayal of an actual scene or event?*

No.

Checkpoints 5 and 7 do not apply.

SOURCE C

An engraving showing an Irish eviction, The Illustrated London News, *15 January 1887*

1 *Does the picture attempt realistically to portray people, events, buildings, etc., or does it poke fun at them by means of a cartoon or an exaggerated drawing (called a caricature)?*

It is a very realistic picture, but obviously it has been carefully composed to make a strong and dramatic effect.

2 *What does the picture show? What does it tell us about the past?*

It shows the eviction of an old man, a woman and baby, and a small girl from a cottage in County Kerry during the Irish Troubles of the late 1880s. It highlights the harsh use the British government made of troops and police to enforce the rights of the landlords against their tenants in Ireland.

3 *When was the picture drawn? Was it drawn at roughly the same time as the event or feature it depicts? Is it a primary source?*

It is a primary source drawn in 1886 or 1887.

4 *Why was the picture drawn or painted? Was it simply an illustration (e.g. to accompany a news item or to illustrate a book), or is there any reason to think the artist was using the picture to make you feel in a certain way about the events or people depicted?*

The picture illustrated a news item about evictions in Ireland. Most people sympathised with the evicted tenants rather than with the landlords. This is why the look in the old man's eyes was drawn to excite sympathy. So, too, was the plight of the young grandchildren and their mother.

6   *Even if it looks like a realistic picture, is there any reason to think it is a product of the artist's imagination rather than a portrayal of an actual scene or event?*

The dramatic nature of the illustration suggests that the artist may have used his imagination. Although it was drawn by A. Forestier (you can see his name in the bottom left-hand corner) the caption in *The Illustrated London News* says that it is 'From a sketch by our special artist'. In other words Forestier drew this picture in his English studio from a sketch supplied by another artist in Ireland!

Checkpoints 5 and 7 do not apply.

EXERCISES AND ACTIVITIES

The Dinner Hour, Wigan

This picture was painted in 1874 by the painter Eyre Crowe. It was probably posed and painted in his studio. The artist may well have used sketches made in the streets of Wigan before working on the painting. It may or may not depict actual mills and factories.

1   *Go through the checklist on page 81. What value would you put on this painting as a source of historical information?*

'Lost in London', The
Illustrated London
News, 7 January 1888

Punch cartoon,
22 September 1888

BLIND-MAN'S BUFF

Two entirely different attitudes to the London Metropolitan Police are depicted in these two drawings, both dating from the same year, 1888. The cartoon, 'Blind-man's buff' reflected the impatience and fear of members of the public at Scotland Yard's inability to find the Jack the Ripper murderer.

2   *Go through the checklist on page 81 with each of the pictures. What value would you put on each one as a source of historical information? What does it tell you about the attitudes of people in Victorian London to the police?*

FACTS FROM PHOTOGRAPHS

Kelvedon, Essex in about 1850

Look at this photograph. Here recorded for all time are just a few seconds of a sunny summer's day sometime in the early 1850s. At this time there were public executions in Britain; Africa was still largely unexplored; Queen Victoria was a young woman in her early thirties; it was not yet compulsory to go to school.

Nearly 140 years have passed since then. Yet you can still capture the excitement of these villagers in Kelvedon in Essex. Perhaps some of them were seeing a camera for the very first time. It is not hard to imagine the photographer who took the photograph – buried inside a deep black cape, focusing the huge box-like camera mounted on a heavy tripod in the middle of the road. Traffic was not a problem on country roads in those days!

When we look at a photograph like this we are like eyewitnesses. It is true we do not see the picture in colour. Nor do we see the movement in the scene. But there are clues in the photograph which we can use to find out more about the scene it portrays.

Notice how the people in the photograph are all facing the camera. Notice, too, that the horses are blurred. This is because it took several seconds to take a photograph with the earliest cameras. Action photographs were not possible then. This is why most photographs were carefully posed. People took up positions they could hold for several seconds at a time. They knew they were being photographed.

Look at the short shadows on the ground. The photograph could not have been taken in winter. Shadows like these help you to judge the season of the year when a photograph was taken. Photographers had to take their photographs when the sun was at its height – at midday. In Britain shadows as short as this are thrown by the sun only at midday in summer. Yet everyone is wearing heavy clothes!

We have no precise date for this photograph but there is a clue which tells us the photograph was taken in the period between about 1845 and 1860. Three of the men in the photograph are wearing distinctive tall hats, called stovepipe hats, which were only worn during this period.

Picture clues like these can help you to make better use of the photographs you see from the past. But bear in mind that although a photograph can give you the impression of being an eyewitness, it is far from certain that what it shows is a fair representation of reality itself. Most photographers carefully select the best viewpoints for their photographs if they can. They, *not* the camera, decide what the photograph will show! This photograph may or may not be typical of Kelvedon. It may or may not be typical of a Victorian village in about 1850. Questions like these can be answered only by studying other photographs and comparing them with pictures and written accounts.

Bear in mind, too, that the camera can also lie. Photographs are sometimes altered to improve the appearance of the people shown in the pictures or to block out something which spoils the view. Some photographs have even been deliberately faked.

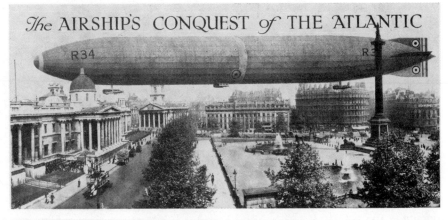

This photograph, showing the immense size of the R34 airship, was printed in The Graphic *on 12 July 1919. How do you think the photograph was taken?*

The first cameras were very heavy and cumbersome. They were also expensive and, as you have seen, recorded anything that moved as a blur on the photograph. Photographers needed good sunlight to take good photographs. This is one reason why it is difficult to find photographs of Victorian slums which match the appalling conditions described by writers such as Henry Mayhew or Charles Dickens. The slums were dark and gloomy. They were crowded with people. They were also dangerous places for the wealthy to set up their expensive cameras! It was only the invention of the Kodak camera using rollfilm in 1889 and the development of fast shutter speeds which enabled photographers to take candid (unposed) photographs without being observed.

Checklist — **Photographs**

1   *What does the photograph show? What does it tell us about the past?*

2   *When and where was the photograph taken? If no date is given, use clues to estimate the date.*

3   *Why was the photograph taken? Is there any reason to think the photographer chose a viewpoint or a subject to make us feel in a certain way about the event or people depicted?*

4   *Is there any sign that the people in the photograph are posing for the photographer? Were they aware of the camera? Does this make any difference to the value of the photograph?*

5   *Is there any reason to think that the photograph is not a typical example of what it appears to show? Is there any reason to think that it may have been altered in any way?*

Going through the Checklist

Punch and Judy show (printed in The Queen's Empire *published in 1897)*

1   *What does the photograph show? What does it tell us about the past?*

Children and adults are watching a Punch and Judy show on a street corner in London. The photograph helps to confirm the descriptions of street entertainers to be found in written descriptions of Victorian London. The metropolis had thousands of street entertainers in the years before radio and television. Notice the cobbled street, the gas lamps, the clothes, the horsedrawn delivery van, and the 'To Let' sign.

2 *When and where was the photograph taken? If no date is given, use clues to estimate the date.*

It was taken in a London street in about 1897. Even if we did not know the date of the publication from which the photograph is taken we could estimate the date from the Norfolk jackets worn by some of the boys and the clothes worn by the men, women and girls.

3 *Why was the photograph taken? Is there any reason to think the photographer chose a viewpoint or a subject to make us feel in a certain way about the event or people depicted?*

It seems to be a straightforward illustration of a popular street entertainment typical of Victorian London.

4 *Is there any sign that the people in the photograph are posing for the photographer? Were they aware of the camera? Does this make any difference to the value of the photograph?*

Several children have spotted the photographer but most of the people in the crowd are too busy watching the show. Since there is movement in the photograph but little blurring we can guess that the photograph was taken with one of the new hand-held cameras.

5 *Is there any reason to think that the photograph is not a typical example of what it appears to show? Is there any reason to think that it may have been altered in any way?*

No.

EXERCISES AND ACTIVITIES

Harvest field

Go through the checklist with this photograph and those on page 96. See if you can estimate the date when each was taken. What is their value as sources of historical information?

Street scene outside
the Bank of England

A London horsebus

EVIDENCE IN SOUND AND ON FILM

The first sound recordings were made by Thomas Alva Edison in 1877. The first moving films were made in the 1890s. These two great inventions provided historians with important new sources of evidence. Since they are not in printed form, however, their value in the study of history has not always been appreciated. Only since the coming of television has effective use been made of old film for the benefit of the general public. As a result, people can now see movie film of the funeral of Queen Victoria in 1901 or watch the coronation of Queen Elizabeth II in 1953. Old movie films enable us to see or hear some of the events of history as they happened.

The main drawback to the use of movie film is that it can be easily *edited* (altered) to show whatever the film editor wants us to see. Lengths of movie film can be cut out and then stuck back together in a different order. It is very easy to assume that because the images are moving in a documentary film we are actually seeing events in sequence exactly as they happened at the time. In many cases you are, but you cannot be certain of this! Movie film has been one of the most powerful weapons used by people involved in propaganda (as in Nazi Germany) and in advertising (see also pages 65–72).

On pages 24–7 you saw evidence relating to the death of Emily Wilding Davison after the Epsom Derby on 4 June 1913. A movie film was made of the race and shown at the Palace Theatre in London. This is how a journalist on *The Times* described the film when he saw it shown for the first time on Derby night, 1913.

The tragic incident at the 1913 Derby

A CINEMATOGRAPH VIEW

The scene at Tattenham Corner was shown on the cinematograph at the Palace Theatre last night. Viewed from a point opposite Tattenham Corner the vast crowd was seen with every head turned in the direction from which the horses were coming. A moment later a bunch, so closely packed that it is scarcely possible to distinguish one horse from another, passed at a great pace. There is a pause for a moment, and suddenly a woman is seen to spring forward from behind the white rails, but as she sets foot upon the course two horses come by. There is a flicker and a flash of white, the woman is prostrate on the turf and a jockey is flung head foremost from his mount and lies in a huddled heap a dozen yards from the woman. A moment more and the remaining horses have passed, but the jockey and the woman lie still and silent, and then the great crowd, moved by a common impulse, closes round them.

The Times, Thursday, 5 June 1913

As it happens, the clip of film described in this report has been included in at least one schools broadcast.

To the eyewitnesses at Epsom, glued to the race, the incident, which was over in a flash, came as a complete and unexpected shock. It was unthinkable that anyone would actually want to run on to the track during the race. Not surprisingly, they had different versions of what happened in the midst of the confusion.

The modern viewer of a movie film shown on a video recorder has no such excuse. Slow motion and the rewind button can be used to get an instant replay of history. In other words you can be an eyewitness to an important historical event, but with the added advantage of being able to repeat the film over and over again until you think you know for sure what happened.

Almost every historian who has ever described this event in print (including the author until he saw the video recording of a schools broadcast!) is on record as saying that Emily Wilding Davison 'threw herself under the King's horse'. As you will recall (pages 24–5), the eyewitnesses at the Derby did not say this, but everyone later assumed that this is what must have happened.

Here is a modern 'eyewitness' account of the 1913 Derby, written after watching about a dozen replays of this incident on a video recorder.

Emily Wilding Davison can be seen clearly ducking under the barrier after the leading horses have passed. She stands upright in the middle of the racecourse, facing the remaining horses in the race. Her arms appear to be stretched outwards. At no time does she fling herself under the hooves of a horse. She seems bewildered, at first, trying to grab at the reins of three horses all close together and passing her far too quickly for her to have any chance of stopping them. Then there is a short gap in the field. It is enough to give her the chance to position herself and reach up to the next horse as it races towards her. She grabs at the reins again but is knocked down and the horse and the jockey also fall. Two other horses ride past as they lie on the ground.

In other words, the 'cinematograph film' proves conclusively that:

- Emily Wilding Davison did not throw herself under the hooves of the King's horse. Far from it. She was standing upright all the time and her only motion when the horse approached was to reach up with her hands towards the reins.

- It was sheer chance that the horse that knocked her down was Anmer, the King's horse. In fact, she tried to stop the earlier horses as soon as she stepped on to the race track.

- Anmer was third from last at Tattenham Corner. It was *not* leading the field, nor was it the last horse in the race. This corrects the statements in Source A on page 24 and in Source D on page 25.

These may seem trivial points but they do have some importance to the history of the suffragette movement. In the first place they suggest that Emily Davison did not really set out to become a martyr at all, although she did want to stop or disrupt the race. In fact she gives every impression of having been taken aback by the speed of the horses. So perhaps she was not quite the heroine and martyr portrayed by the suffragettes in their subsequent literature. Equally she was not the 'half-demented' woman depicted by many commentators and historians both at the time and since.

EXERCISES AND ACTIVITIES

Look closely at clips of old newsreel film on a video recorder or whenever an old documentary film is shown on schools television. Use your eyes and ears to note carefully what happens. Record your observations as an eyewitness would have done had he or she been a witness to the same event.

If possible take the opportunity to view the film of the 1913 Derby. Write your own 'eyewitness' account of the incident and compare it with those printed above on pages 25 and 98.

FACTS FROM STATISTICS

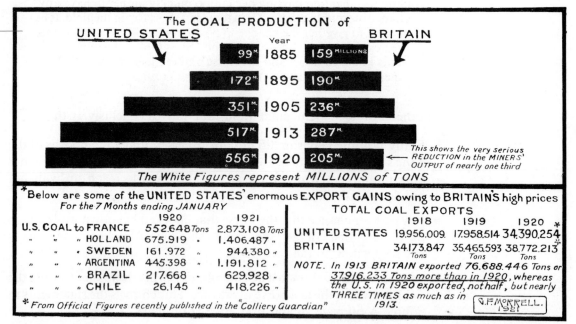

The COAL PRODUCTION of

UNITED STATES   Year   BRITAIN

	Year	
99ᴹ	1885	159 MILLIONS
172ᴹ	1895	190ᴹ
351ᴹ	1905	236ᴹ
517ᴹ	1913	287ᴹ
556ᴹ	1920	205ᴹ

← This shows the very serious REDUCTION in the MINERS' OUTPUT of nearly one third

The White Figures represent MILLIONS of TONS

*Below are some of the UNITED STATES' enormous EXPORT GAINS owing to BRITAIN'S high prices

For the 7 Months ending JANUARY

U.S. COAL to		1920	1921
U.S. COAL to	FRANCE	552.648 Tons	2.873.108 Tons
" "	" HOLLAND	675.919 "	1.406.487 "
" "	• SWEDEN	161.972 "	944.380 "
" "	" ARGENTINA	445.398 "	1.191.812 "
" "	" BRAZIL	217.668 "	629.928 "
" "	" CHILE	26.145 "	418.226 "

TOTAL COAL EXPORTS

	1918	1919	1920
UNITED STATES	19.956.009	17.958.514	34.390.254
BRITAIN	34.173.847	35.465.593	38.772.213
	Tons	Tons	Tons

NOTE. In 1913 BRITAIN exported 76.688.446 Tons or 37.916.233 Tons more than in 1920, whereas the U.S. in 1920 exported, not half, but nearly THREE TIMES as much as in 1913.

*From Official Figures recently published in the "Colliery Guardian"

G.F. MORRELL. 1921

Why do you think this graph and the statistics underneath were published in The Graphic on 14 May 1921, at the time of a coal-miners' strike? What were these statistics designed to show?

Statistics are an important source of information for the historian. The most important sources of statistics in social history are the official census reports which have been published every ten years since the first census in 1801. Official statistics of agricultural and industrial production, length of railway line, number of motor vehicles, numbers of people unemployed, and countless other statistics have also been published at regular intervals. These statistics are invaluable since they help us to measure the progress or decline of industries and the growth or decline of towns.

But there are problems. Some statistics can be misleading. They may have been collected or counted in circumstances which led to inaccuracies. The first census reports were compiled from census returns completed by householders, many of whom were illiterate. Sometimes the statistics are biased. They may also be incomplete.

Many printed statistics, like opinion polls, are based on samples instead of being complete surveys. Statistics for 1755 tell us about 1755. These may or may not be typical of the 1750s as a whole. Statistics for London tell us about London, not about the rest of Britain. Unfortunately, you will rarely have the chance to check for yourself when, how, why and where the statistics were collected, and whether they are reliable.

This is why it is best to treat all statistics with a certain amount of caution and to use them as a guide rather than as proof. In particular, beware of believing statistics just because they back up your own or other people's arguments!

Checklist — **Statistics**

1 *When and how were the statistics collected? Who collected them? Were they in a position to collect accurate or reliable statistics? Can we be certain they are not guesses, estimates, approximations, or even lies?*

2 *Is it likely that someone else working in exactly the same way would collect the same statistics? If not, why not?*

3 *Are the statistics complete or only a sample of all the possible statistics which could have been recorded?*

4 *Who selected the statistics for use and how were they chosen?*

5 *What do the statistics tell you about the past? What do they prove? If they are quoted to back up a statement, do they really support the conclusions drawn from them by the writer?*

6 *Are the statistics used to support a statement which may be biased or prejudiced?*

7 *If averages are used, do they mean anything? See if you can find out how they were calculated.*

Going through the Checklist

Cholera and the Thames
What do you mean by telling me that cholera slew in Rotherhithe its 205 victims in every 10 000, in St Olave's its 181, in St Saviour's its 153, in Lambeth its 120, while in the Strand it carried off only 35, in Kensington 33, in Marylebone 17, and in Hampstead 8, out of the same number.

Extract from *Punch* in the 1850s

1 *When and how were the statistics collected? Who collected them?*

Presumably these are official statistics which were compiled during a cholera epidemic, but we cannot be sure. The absence of a precise date throws some doubt on the reliability of these figures. Nor does the extract indicate the length of time to which these statistics refer.

2 *Is it likely that someone else working in exactly the same way would collect the same statistics? If not, why not?*

If they are official statistics based on medical reports there is no reason to think the totals would be different.

3 *Are the statistics complete or only a sample of all the possible statistics which could have been recorded?*

They are only samples of the death rate from cholera in a number of London boroughs.

4 *Who selected the statistics for use and how were they chosen?*

No information is given, but it seems certain that the statistics were chosen because they showed that the incidence of cholera increased from west to east and with increasing proximity to the River Thames.

5 *What do the statistics tell you about the past? What do they prove? If they are quoted to back up a statement, do they really support the conclusions drawn from them by the writer?*

The statistics show a rapid increase in the number of deaths from cholera in London the nearer someone's home was to the Thames and to the East End. Because *Punch* agitated to clean up the Thames we can assume that these statistics were used to support that campaign. However, they do not *prove conclusively* that there was any direct link between the Thames and the spread of cholera. That could only be proved by medical scientists. But they do throw suspicion on the Thames as a possible, or probable, carrier of disease.

6 *Are the statistics used to support any statement which may be biased or prejudiced?*

Since *Punch* carried on a campaign to improve the quality of the water in the Thames it is likely that any evidence which pointed the finger of suspicion at the river would have been welcomed by the editor (see the cartoons on pages 61 and 63). Accordingly, we may suspect some bias in the selection of the statistics but this does not necessarily mean that the figures are inaccurate.

Checkpoint 7 does not apply.

EXERCISES AND ACTIVITIES

The statistics which follow record some of the prices paid to Henry Purefoy, a Buckinghamshire landowner, in December 1739. He had sold 'goods and chattells' belonging to a Mr Hunt who owed him rent. The prices he received were carefully recorded in his account book, together with the expenses he had had to meet as a result of the sale. The modern metric equivalents are shown in brackets.

December the 5th
Recd of Nathaniell Kinch for 4 Piggs £4 1s 0d [£4.05]
December the 10th
Recd of Thos. Emerton for a cow and 2 Heifers [young cows] £7 2s 6s [£7.13]
Recd of Goodman William Hobcraft for a cow and a bull £5 5s 0d [£5.25]
Recd of Goodman Barns for a cow £3 5s 0d [£3.25]

Recd of a Stranger man for a cow £3 12s 6d [£3.63]
Recd of my mother Purefoy for 22 sheep £9 2s 6d [£9.13]

Paid William Strange for crying a sale of Mr Hunt's cattle at
Brackley Market 4d [2p]. Paid young George Penell for crying a
sale of Mr Hunt's cattle at Buckingham Market 4d [2p].

The Purefoy Letters, edited by G. Eland, 1931

1   *Go through the checklist for statistics on page 101.*

2   *How did Mr Purefoy advertise that he had cattle for sale?*

3   *What was the approximate price of a cow in Buckinghamshire in December 1739?*

4   *Using your answer to question 3, work out the approximate price of (a) a bull, (b) a heifer.*

5   *What was the approximate price of (a) a sheep, (b) a pig?*

6   *Name any possible drawbacks to the use of these statistics as a guide to cattle, sheep and pig prices in Britain as a whole in the eighteenth century.*

In 1910 Dr Newman, the Chief Medical Officer of the Board of Education, published his official report on the health of children in Britain's public elementary schools. This was the first time anyone had made a survey of this type. His report was made possible because the systematic medical inspection of every schoolchild had been ordered following the passing of the Health Inspection Act by the Liberal government of 1907. This is how a newspaper report summed up his findings.

The Report throws an appalling light upon the absolute amount of disease from which the children now at school are suffering ... Ten per cent suffer from defective sight, three to five per cent from defective hearing, eight per cent from adenoid growths obstructive of proper breathing, twenty to forty per cent from unclean heads, and about one per cent from ringworm, tuberculosis, and heart disease.

The Times, 30 November 1910

7   *Go through the checklist for statistics on page 101.*

8   *Who do you think collected these statistics in the first place? Is there any chance that they were mistaken?*

9   *Suggest reasons which might account for these 'appalling' figures. Why do you think The Times was surprised by these figures?*

10   *Show these statistics in the form of a graph.*

Working as a Historian

SIMILARITIES AND DIFFERENCES

Similarity does not mean 'the same'. It means that things are alike in certain respects but not identical. This is an important difference. Two mill towns may look alike to an outsider but they may be very different places to the people who actually live there.

In fact every historical event is unique. There is nothing quite like it. This is why it is often much easier to detect differences than it is to find similarities. Nonetheless there are patterns in history. A revolution in one country may be followed by similar revolutions in neighbouring countries. The growth of industry in Britain in the eighteenth and nineteenth centuries was followed by similar, but different, patterns of industrial growth in other countries in Europe.

If you are asked to look for similarities or differences in history you may be asked to compare two or three written extracts or a number of pictures or photographs. You will need to pick out the important things that matter, not the minor details. If you jot down the main similarities and differences first of all, you can use these lists later on to help plan your answer.

EXERCISES AND ACTIVITIES

Look at the two accounts which follow. Both describe living and working conditions on the coalfields towards the end of the nineteenth century. Both extracts come from articles printed in popular monthly magazines of the day. Source A was published in 1882 and Source B seven years later in 1889. Source A was written by Thomas Burt who was the Liberal MP for a coal-mining constituency – Morpeth in Northumberland. Source B is by a writer called G. Blake Walker.

SOURCE A

The hours now worked by adults underground in Northumberland are from seven to eight per day. The work is exceedingly hard, and most of those who have seen how the work is done will consider the hours quite long enough ... In Northumberland and Durham, the custom from time immemorial has been for the colliery owner to supply a free house to the workman, this being counted part of his wages. Until recently many of these houses were very inferior, a great number of them consisting of a single room and a garret. At the newer collieries, however, a much better class of house has been built; and during the prosperous times of a few years ago, many of the colliery proprietors spent large sums in improving the house accommodation. Now many of the colliery houses are really excellent. Yet there are still some which are utterly unfit for human habitation; and in certain cases the workmen have to pay their own rent for very inferior houses.

Thomas Burt, *Cassell's Family Magazine*, 1882

SOURCE B

Arrived at the pit-bottom it is some time before the eye accustoms itself to the gloom, the men employed seem weird, dusky-looking beings, moving hither and thither in the dark caverns which open out on either hand...The collier's work is not without its recommendations. The hours are short, the conditions of work are equable; he is independent of the weather and he is well paid. To the danger of accident he is certainly exposed, but, according to statistics, his calling is not so fatal as some others carried on in open day...The colliery is usually surrounded by a number of cottages. These vary as to accommodation and comfort, the newer houses being generally commodious and well arranged. The colliers have each a garden plot which they cultivate.

G. Blake Walker, *The English Illustrated Magazine*, 1889

This engraving is an artist's impression of the interior of a miner's cottage in South Wales in 1873. It was drawn at the time of a coal-miners' strike and appeared on the front page of The Illustrated London News *on 18 January 1873.*

1   *Use the checklist on page 53 to check out Sources A and B first of all. Are they primary sources? Are they eyewitness accounts? Which parts of these extracts are facts and which are opinions?*

2   *Are there any major points on which both writers agree? What are the main similarities?*

3   *What are the main differences between the two sources? How significant are these differences?*

4   *Suggest possible reasons to account for any differences you have noted. Is either writer biased? Did one writer have a better chance of finding out than the other?*

5   *Does the engraving support or contradict the information contained in Sources A and B?*

The account which follows also describes the life and work of a coal miner but it was written in 1897 – fifteen years after Source A and eight years after Source B.

SOURCE C

I know a great deal about the miner and his life. I have seen him at work, toiling hour after hour in the deep recesses of a mine; I have seen him risking his life to save that of others ... As a rule, the miner is improvident. He earns good wages, and while he is content to live in miserable jerry-built cottages he squanders his money in betting and even worse pleasures ... After a man has been down in the darkness of a pit for eight or ten hours, breathing obnoxious gases and lying in uncomfortable postures working at the coal face ... it is no wonder that at the close of the day he prefers the jovial rowdy companionship of his mates to study ... I have been down coal mines 1000 feet below the surface, mines into which there is running a constant stream of water and where the seam of coal is only three or four feet [about a metre] thick; I have crawled for a couple of miles along these seams till my back has ached and when I have come to an open space I could hardly straighten myself up; I have tramped slush ... and been choked with fumes; I have watched men, stripped naked to the waist, hewing at the coal while the lamps have flickered faintly upon their dust and perspiration-streaked chests.

J.F. Fraser, 'Life in a Coal Mine' from *Windsor Magazine*, 1897

6   *Use the checklist on page 53 to check out this source. Is it a primary source? Is it an eyewitness report? Which parts are facts and which are opinions?*

7   *Make a list of the ways in which this extract is similar to, and the ways in which it differs from, first Source A and then Source B. How do you account for these differences?*

8 *With which of the two other sources do you think Source C has more in common? Why?*

9 *In what ways do the illustrations of a Scottish colliery accident below add to the information you have obtained from the three extracts in this section?*

Scenes at Blantyre Colliery near Glasgow after a pit explosion in 1877, The Illustrated London News, *3 November 1877*

10 *Which of the three extracts do you think you would pick if you had to choose a reliable description of living and working conditions on the coalfields in the late nineteenth century? Give reasons to explain your choice.*

HOW THINGS CHANGE

Look at this pair of pictures of Fleet Street in London. You can tell they are from the same viewpoint if you look at the position of the church spire against the dome of St Paul's Cathedral. What changes took place between 1848 and 1980? What things remained much the same? Write a paragraph commenting on the changes to Fleet Street in the last hundred years.

An engraving of Fleet Street, London, The Illustrated London News, *8 January 1848*

How and why things change is of great interest to historians. Sometimes the changes are abrupt and clear cut, such as the sudden change in policy which happens when a revolutionary government seizes power. Changes of equal or greater significance in the lives of ordinary people also take place but often slowly, over periods of many years. This was the case with the Agricultural Revolution in Britain which began in the seventeenth century or even earlier.

Despite these changes, many things – such as people's attitudes, customs and traditions – remain much the same. This is called *continuity*. Change and continuity can both be identified when you make comparisons over a period of time.

Some changes, such as those which have dramatically altered the educational system in the last 150 years, have taken place in sudden

A photograph of Fleet Street, London in about 1980

jumps, sometimes backwards, mostly forwards. Other dramatic changes, such as changes in men's and women's fashions, may appear to be important at the time but have little lasting significance. Some of these changes, however, show how attitudes changed. The growing freedom of women in the early twentieth century was marked by the changeover from long, full-length skirts in 1916 to short knee-high skirts some ten years later.

Checklist — Change

Use these checkpoints if you are asked to identify changes which may have taken place.

1 *What was the nature of the change? Was it part of a much bigger change?*

2 *Was it an important and significant change? Did it affect everybody and almost every activity, like the coming of the railway, motor car and telephone? Or did it just affect a section of the community, such as the effect of the means test in the 1930s on the unemployed?*

3 *Who or what benefited from the change? Who or what suffered from the change?*

4 *Did the change take place suddenly, rapidly, steadily, slowly, jerkily, or imperceptibly?*

5 *Did the change affect people mainly because of its social effects, such as on education or health; or mainly because of its economic effects, such as on agriculture or industry; or both?*

Going through the Checklist

Read this account of farming in Britain in 1846. It is just one of the many sources of evidence which you could use to identify some of the changes which took place on Britain's farms during the Agricultural Revolution. The writer compares the way of life of a gentleman farmer and his family with that of their ancestors a hundred years earlier.

Then, the farmer, dressed plainly in homespun woollen, toiled with his labourers, sat and generally ate with them in the kitchen, and altogether led a simple life, little exalted above that of his hinds [labourers]. His sons took their regular share of out-door labour, his wife and daughters attended to the kitchen, spun, managed the poultry and dairy, and were generally the first on the harvest-field.

Now, the farmer and his family dress expensively; his duty is to conduct, not to labour with his own hands; he never mingles with his servants unless to direct; his sons are beginning to be educated in those sciences necessary to the perfection of their art; his daughters are taught every accomplishment of modern education, take no share in the labour of the farm, and only attend to such household duties as devolve upon ladies in town. The farmer keeps his thoroughbred horse or drives his own curricle [a form of carriage]; attends market as a merchant does the Exchange; transacts his business not as of old with the consumer, but with the cornfactor, thereby saving time, and avoiding expense and trouble.

Chambers's Journal, 11 July 1846

'The Cockney Farmer' – a cartoon drawn by George Cruikshank in 1835. He was making fun of the newly rich manufacturers and merchants who had bought estates in the country. The cockney farmer in the cartoon has dragged his friends 'through Mud and Mire' to see his handiwork. 'I made every bit of this dung myself.' How was this type of gentleman farmer different from the one described in the extract?

1 *What was the nature of the change? Was it part of a much bigger change?*

The writer argues that the well-to-do farmer and his family had changed from being working (yeoman) farmers to becoming gentleman farmers. The Victorians would have said that the yeoman farmer had changed from being working class to being middle class. The farmer was now an employer not a labourer. His children went to good schools. He kept a carriage. He thought of himself as a businessman rather than as a farmer. This change was just one of the features of the Agricultural Revolution in Britain in the period between 1750 and 1850.

2 *Was it an important and significant change? Did it affect everybody and almost every activity? Or did it affect just a section of the community?*

The extract *suggests* that it was a universal change, but from other sources you will discover that it only affected large farms. Small farmers continued to work alongside their labourers.

3 *Who or what benefited from the change? Who or what suffered from the change?*

Obviously the farmer and his family benefited since they lived a more luxurious and leisured life. The main sufferers were the labourers, since these changes created a gulf between the farmer and his workers. A farmer who did not work in the fields with his labourers could hardly be expected to understand their problems.

4 *Did the change take place suddenly, rapidly, steadily, slowly, jerkily, or imperceptibly?*

There is nothing in the extract to indicate the rate of change but we can guess that it took place slowly over a period of many years.

5 *Did the change affect people mainly because of its social effects, such as on education or health; or mainly because of its economic effects, such as on agriculture or industry; or both?*

As you can see from the extract, it did both. It changed the relationship between the farmer and his workers and it also turned many farms into businesses. Farmers made higher profits by using machines and by introducing scientific methods of farming. This meant that they needed to employ fewer farmworkers on their farms.

EXERCISES AND ACTIVITIES

Read this extract from *A Tour Through the Whole Island of Great Britain* by Daniel Defoe, which was first published in the 1720s.

> We see several villages, formerly standing, as it were, in the country, and at a great distance, now joined to the streets by continued buildings, and more making haste to meet in the like manner; for example, Deptford, this town was formerly reckoned, at least two miles off from Redriff [Rotherhithe], and that over the marshes too, a place unlikely ever to be inhabited; and yet now, by the increase of buildings in that town itself, and the many streets erected at Redriff, and by the docks and building-yards on the riverside, which stand between both, the town of Deptford, and the streets of Redriff, or Rotherhith (as they write it!) are effectually joined, and the building daily increasing;

1 *Go through the checklist. What does Defoe tell you about the growth of London in the early eighteenth century? What changes had taken place?*

An engraving of Bolton
Town Hall, The
Illustrated London
News, 7 June 1873

A photograph of
Bolton Town Hall in
1973

2 Compare this modern photograph of Bolton Town Hall in Lancashire with
the engraving which was drawn in June 1873 and published two days
after the town hall had been opened by the Prince of Wales. What
changes took place between 1873 and 1973? What remained much the
same? Go through the checklist and comment on the similarities and
differences you notice.

IMAGINING THE PAST

Trying to imagine what it was like to live in the past is called historical *empathy*. It is a way of trying to understand why people behaved in the past in the way they did. Instead of judging their actions by our own standards we look at events through the eyes of the people living at that time.

Really understanding what happened in the past will only come about if you can set aside your own ideas and background and picture yourself in the past. How would you have behaved then? A good way of imagining yourself in the past is to think of everything in the present tense! What do you think of Humphry Davy's new safety lamp in 1820? What are you going to do when the open fields in your village are enclosed in 1760?

Another way of getting a vivid picture of what it was really like to live in the past is to read accounts and stories which tell you how people spoke and how they behaved. Look closely at old pictures and especially at old photographs. When you see a photograph of a Victorian or an Edwardian street, for instance, try to imagine what it would have been like to be there when the photographer took the picture.

EXERCISES AND ACTIVITIES

A Victorian street

1 *You can see what the people, vehicles and buildings look like in the photograph opposite. Now imagine the atmosphere as well. What can you smell? What can you hear? Are the people near you rich or poor? What are their clothes like? Are they educated? How do they speak? Are they well fed? Are they hungry? Where do they live? What jobs have they got? Are they well behaved? How do their lives differ from yours today?*

Look at Sources A, B, C and D. The engravings A and C were printed in a popular weekly magazine to draw attention to the appalling conditions to be seen in the slums of Victorian London at that time. Each engraving shown here is followed by an extract from the long written description which accompanied the picture when it was published in the 1850s.

SOURCE A

Outside a public house in 1856, The Illustrated London News, *6 December 1856*

SOURCE B

SUNDAY MORNING in the low neighbourhoods of London. Such idle men, such slatternly [slovenly] women, and such ragged, unkempt [untidy] children crowd round the closed doors of the public-houses and loll against the walls, or play in the gutters ...

The dwellers in country places and small cities have no idea how the lives of hundreds of thousands pent up in London are spent and wasted. There is little or no escape for these poor creatures into better scenes than their own alleys, courts, and lanes, fetid [rotting] and vile, in spite of sanitary laws and street scavengers.

Surely it is not keeping the Sabbath holy to compel men to mix in such scenes; and yet, shameful as the confession is, there is little or nothing done to find them better pleasures or better teaching.

The Illustrated London News, 6 December 1856

SOURCE C

The King's Arms Yard,
Coal-Yard, Drury Lane,
London, The Illustrated
London News,
22 October 1853

SOURCE D

The unwholesome condition of the dwellings of the poor in London and other large towns is a fearful source of evil. Our Illustration represents an actual example of too many lodgings which are still to be found in London in spite of the regulations of the police. Let us consider a house, with floor above floor, packed as shown in the Engraving; the cellars filled with either refuse or wretched inmates – the ventilation shocking – the drainage bad – the parts adjoining filled with filth and refuse – these spread over many parts – and who can wonder at the visitation of fever and cholera ... These people are too poor to pay for proper lodgings. Can no means be found of lodging them and their families in a wholesome manner at a small yet remunerating cost?

A worse sanitary state of things could not well be than that in the neighbourhood of the Coal-Yard, Drury Lane. Here are from sixteen to eighteen large families living in small inconvenient apartments, above cow-sheds, donkey and horse stables &c. Sometimes many cartloads of refuse are allowed to remain in the yard; the pavement is uneven, and filled here and there with stagnant water. It is shocking to see the squalid children attempting to play in such a place; and yet this place is within a stone's throw of the spot on which the Great Plague broke out [in 1665 with the loss of over 100 000 people].

The Illustrated London News, 22 October 1853

2 Use the checklists on pages 53 and 81 to check through these extracts and their accompanying engravings.

3 Imagine that you are living in the King's Arms Yard in 1853. What do you look like? What clothes are you wearing? When did you last wash? When did you last eat? What can you smell? What can you see? What can you hear? Imagine what the King's Arms Yard looks like and what you feel like when it is pouring with rain. What is it like when it is hot in summer? What is it like in the middle of the night? Write a vivid description in your own words entitled 'My Life in the King's Arms Yard'.

4 What improvement was the writer of Source B hoping for? What improvement was the writer of Source D hoping for?

CAUSE AND CONSEQUENCE

A London factory scene 'on Monday at noon' (above) and the same factory area 'on a Sunday morning' (below). What cause and what consequence are illustrated in these photographs printed in The Graphic on 15 October 1921? What do they tell you about the effect of industry on the environment nearly seventy years ago?

Whenever we look at how things change (see pages 108–113) we also look at the causes and consequences of making those changes.

Scientists in certain subjects, such as physics and chemistry, can usually find out for certain why a change occurs. They can repeat an experiment over and over again until they are satisfied with the result. As a result, they know that if they repeat the cause (such as adding sulphuric acid to zinc) they will always get the same result or consequence (zinc sulphate and hydrogen). In history there is no such certainty.

Politicians argue that in appearing to give in to Hitler at Munich in 1938, the British prime minister, Neville Chamberlain, only encouraged the Nazis to invade Poland in 1939. A policy like this, of giving way to a dictator, is called *appeasement*. Munich has since been used as a reason for acting toughly today. In other words, many politicians believe that aggression is the inevitable consequence of a policy of appeasement.

In fact, the Munich Crisis was unique. It is by no means certain that a similar consequence would follow in different circumstances, with another dictator, at another date, in another country. History is not like that. It can show people what happened in the past. It can teach them to learn from their past mistakes. But it cannot lay down strict laws like those you may have learned in science.

For one thing, it is often difficult to tell which is the cause and which is the consequence. Which came first, the chicken or the egg? Did the Industrial Revolution help to cause a rise in the birth rate (because it created an increased demand for factory workers)? Or did the rise in the birth rate help to cause the Industrial Revolution (because many more people needed jobs)? This is why we have to be very careful in history when we talk of cause and effect or cause and consequence.

Checklist — Cause and Consequence

Use these checkpoints when you study cause and consequence.

1   *What are the suggested effects and consequences?*

2   *Are these effects and consequences facts which can be proved or disproved? Or are they opinions? For instance, the statement that 'the population of London trebled in size between 1851 and 1931' is a consequence which can be easily proved if you look at the census statistics. But the statement that 'young people were better behaved fifty years ago' is an opinion. It cannot be proved or disproved to everyone's satisfaction.*

3   *What causes of these effects and consequences have been given?*

4   *Which of these causes can be backed up by facts and evidence? Can they be proved or disproved?*

Going through the Checklist

The following extract is from evidence that Professor Lyon Playfair, a noted British scientist, gave to the Schools Inquiry Commission in 1867. He said that he had asked a number of fellow experts at an industrial exhibition in Paris why there had been a decline in British 'inventiveness and progress in industry' since 1862. This was his summary of their replies.

> The one cause upon which there was most unanimity of conviction is that France, Prussia, Austria, Belgium and Switzerland possess good systems of industrial education for the masters and managers of factories and workshops, and that England has none. A second cause was also generally, though not so universally, admitted, that we had suffered from the want of cordiality [lack of good feeling] between the employers of labour and workmen, engendered [caused] by the numerous strikes, and more particularly by that rule of many Trades' Unions that men shall work upon an average ability, without giving free scope to the skill and ability which they may individually possess.

1   *What are the suggested effects and consequences?*

Dr Playfair claimed that there had been a decline in British inventiveness and progress in industry between 1862 and 1867.

2   *Are these effects and consequences facts which can be proved or disproved? Or are they opinions?*

They are opinions not facts. It is very difficult indeed to prove a decline in something you cannot actually see, hear or touch! A decline in inventiveness cannot be measured. Nor can a lack of progress in industry. Professor Playfair did not mean a decline in industrial output (which could be measured). He meant a lack of progress in developing new technology.

3   *What causes of these effects and consequences have been given?*

(a)   Lack of effective industrial education in Britain compared with other countries in Europe.

(b)   Lack of co-operation between workers and employers caused by strikes and the insistence of the trade unions on standard rates of pay and standard working conditions.

4   *Which of these causes can be backed up by facts and evidence? Can they be proved or disproved?*

(a)   It was certainly a fact that Britain lacked an effective system of industrial education in the 1860s compared with other countries in Europe. But this does not explain why Britain earlier took the lead in the development of industry, transport and agriculture. There was no lack of inventiveness when the steam engines of

Newcomen and Watt were invented; nor at the time of Darby, Cort, Huntsman, Bessemer, Wedgwood, Kay, Hargreaves, Arkwright, Crompton, Cartwright, Brunel, Trevithick, and George and Robert Stephenson.

(b)   The trade unions are often blamed for lack of progress in industry – a matter of opinion rather than a matter of fact. As it happens, one of the most damaging strikes of the 1860s was at Sheffield, where the unions were striking for safer and better working conditions in the cutlery industries. This was hardly a hindrance to progress in industry.

EXERCISES AND ACTIVITIES

Read the two extracts on the next page from *A Tour Through the Whole Island of Great Britain* by Daniel Defoe, which was first published in the 1720s. In the first extract (Source A) Defoe describes the effect of the woollen industry on the towns of the West Country near Cirencester and Bath. In the second extract (Source B) he describes the effect that the improvements to the roads had had on the growth of London.

Hand wheel spinners in the domestic woollen industry

SOURCE A ... innumerable villages, hamlets, and scattered houses, in which, generally speaking, the spinning work of all this manufacture is performed by the poor people; the master clothiers who generally live in the greater towns, sending out the wool weekly to their houses, by their servants and horses, and at the same time, bringing back the yarn that they have spun and finished, which then is fitted for the loom. The increasing and flourishing circumstances of this trade are happily visible by the great concourse of people to, and increase of buildings and inhabitants in these principal clothing towns where this trade is carried on, and wealth of the clothiers.

SOURCE B This improving of the roads is an infinite improvement to the towns near London, in the convenience of coming to them, which makes the citizens flock out in greater numbers than ever to take lodgings and country-houses, which many, whose business called them often to London, could not do, because of the labour of riding forward and backward, when the roads were but a little dirty, and this is seen in the difference in the rents of the houses in those villages upon such repaired roads, from the rents of the like dwellings and lodgings in other towns of equal distance, where they want those helps, and particularly the increase of the number of buildings in those towns, as above.

1   *Go through the checklist on page 118 for each of these sources.*

2   *What did Defoe say were the effects and consequences caused by the growth of the woollen industry in the West Country by 1720?*

3   *What were the effects and consequences caused by the new road improvements around London by 1720?*

Houses in Wimpole Street and Devonshire Place on the outskirts of London in 1720

SELECTING RELEVANT INFORMATION

Selecting relevant information means selecting only those facts, opinions, judgements and ideas which relate specifically to the subject you are studying.

It is interesting to know that Florence Nightingale was called Florence because she was born in Florence in Italy. But this information is irrelevant if you are studying her work as a nurse. It *is* relevant, however, if you are writing the story of her life. It is easy to be side-tracked in this way. This is why you should always try to make an effort to stick to the subject. Only use information which throws light on your topic.

EXERCISES AND ACTIVITIES

The following extract is from a newspaper account of the trial of a young man who had been accused of breaking the new Combination Laws in 1825. These new Combination Laws actually made it easier for trade unions to operate. The old Combination Acts, passed in 1799 and 1800, had effectively banned trade unions since workers could be sent to prison for attending strike meetings or for 'combining' with other workers to force an employer to raise wages or improve working conditions. In this account of the trial of Robert Ford you can find out how the new Combination Laws worked.

> Friday, a young man, named Robert Ford, a journeyman shoemaker, was brought up on a warrant charged under the New Act, with endeavouring by threats and intimidation, to prevent one George Turner, from returning to his work.
>
> It appeared that all the men in the employment of Mr Ashenden, a boot and shoemaker, at Hampstead, struck for wages about a fortnight ago. Among the rest were the above-named Ford and Turner. The latter, however, was compelled by the rest to strike against his will; and when the whole party were assembled at a public house debating the matter, he said he was sorry he had left his work, and would return to it; upon which Ford, who was one of the most active promoters of the 'strike' swore, that if he did he would drag him through a pond. This was the 'threat and intimidation' complained of.
>
> Ford, in defence, said he made use of no threat. The words he made use of were these:- 'If you return to your work, you ought to be dragged through a pond.'
>
> Mr Halls [the magistrate] said, Turner had sworn otherwise.
>
> Mr Ashenden said, he should not have brought the prisoner here, but this was not a solitary instance of his having used threats to other men.
>
> Mr Halls said, he certainly should put the act in force against the prisoner. Even now he did it with reluctance, but some check must

be put upon the dangerous spirit which seemed to prevail. For the instruction of those whom he saw within hearing he would read that part of one clause of the recent act, which applied to the present case. It stated 'that if any person shall by violence to the person or property, or by threats or intimidation, or by molesting or in any way obstructing another, force or endeavour to force, any journeyman, manufacturer, etc., to depart from his business, or to return his work before it is finished, or preventing any person from returning to his work, etc., every person so offending, or aiding, or assisting therein, shall be imprisoned for any period not exceeding three months'. The act left it to the discretion of the Magistrates whether the hard labour should be added to the imprisonment. The prisoner was sentenced to one month's imprisonment but not to hard labour.

The Age, Sunday, 17 July 1825

1   Is this a primary source? Is it an eyewitness account? Go through the master checklist on page 129.

2   Why was Robert Ford sent to prison? Was it because he went on strike or because he organised the strike? Search through this passage and find the relevant part of the evidence and the relevant part of the Combination Laws which sent him to prison for one month.

3   Which of the following did the new Combination Laws prohibit:
    (a)   going on strike
    (b)   standing in the path of someone wishing to return to work
    (c)   threatening a fellow worker
    (d)   peaceful picketing (i.e. asking fellow workers not to go back to work)
    (e)   erecting a barrier across the entrance to the works to stop people returning to work?

FOR AND AGAINST

A *reasoned argument* is one in which each stage of the argument follows from the preceding one. It uses good reasons to argue the case for or against. The reasons are good because they are based on known facts rather than on bias, prejudice or inaccurate facts. Use this checklist when you examine the arguments in any historical source.

Checklist — A Reasoned Argument

1   List the arguments for.

2   List the arguments against.

3   Which of these arguments are based on facts and which are opinions? Which can be proved? Which are unprovable?

4   Which arguments seem to you to be backed up by the most convincing evidence? Which arguments are weak and unconvincing? Which side has the better case?

EXERCISES AND ACTIVITIES

The extracts that follow are taken from an article by Frederick Ryland in the magazine *The Girl's Own Paper* on 16 May 1896, several years before the founding of the suffragette movement. The article was the fourth in a series entitled 'Politics for Girls'. ('Suffrage' simply means the right to vote; 'Franchise' is another word meaning much the same thing.)

Frederick Ryland concluded that 'if women want the franchise they will have to ask for it, and that in a much more extended fashion than they have at present shown any inclination to do'. Perhaps some of the later suffragettes read his article as girls in 1896 and took heed of his advice ten years later, when they broke up meetings and made it crystal clear to an unwilling government that they wanted the franchise.

Whatever you think of Ryland's arguments, the extract has some value since it indicates some of the prevailing attitudes to women's suffrage at that time.

The arguments he used fell naturally into two groups because he started his article with the points he could find in favour of women's suffrage. He concluded with the arguments against. You will see that he omitted some of the most telling arguments which were used by the suffragists at that time. For one thing women already had the same right as men to vote in local elections for district councils, boards of guardians (responsible for the workhouse system) and for school boards (responsible at that time for state-maintained schools). But they did not have the right to vote for a Member of Parliament. Many well-to-do women paid rates on their houses and taxes on their incomes. Although they could hire, sack, and pay the wages of their footmen, gardeners and coachmen, they could not enter a polling booth and vote with their employees at an election.

FEMALE SUFFRAGE

- Men and women certainly do not entirely understand each other's point of view, and there are many questions, some great and some small, in which women as a rule take a line of their own.
- Then there is the argument for justice. Why should a person otherwise qualified be refused a vote simply on the ground of sex? Mr A at No. 1 has a vote; Mrs B at No. 2, with equal education, and an equal stake in the country, is refused a vote, merely because she is a woman. This seems on the face of it to be an outrage on fairness. But, as a matter of fact, things are usually worse, since Mrs B's gardener or coachman will probably have a vote, while she is without one.
- It is not at all clear that the great majority of women who would obtain the franchise would care to use it. There seems to be no general and wide demand for it.

- Probably not ten per cent of the female voters would on a purely political question go to the poll. It would require some very stimulating appeal, some harrowing attack on the sentimental side, to induce them to vote in large numbers; but when they did vote, the rush would in many constituencies entirely overwhelm the male voters. Now, it cannot be for the advantage of the State that a large body of voters, who habitually take little interest in political matters and do not get the political training which comes from incessant discussion, should be able to rush in and form a momentary and irresponsible majority.
- Suppose, for instance, the vast majority of men were in favour of a war with Russia, and the women vetoed it, or vice versa; in either case it would be felt that as the men supply by far the greater part of the blood and the treasure which would be spent on a war, and out of all comparison in a better position to judge of the effect of such a war on the honour, welfare, and commerce of the country, with them must rest the final decision.
- The truth is that the intelligence even of highly intelligent women is not political. Only a few will take interest in politics steadily and continuously.
- The factory-girl class will be by far the most important class of women voters. The married woman who has no separate house property will have no vote ... Political power in many large cities would be chiefly in the hands of young, ill-educated, giddy, and often ill-conducted girls, living in lodgings.
- As rights of citizenship can hardly be conferred without corresponding duties, the franchise would probably be accompanied by the obligation to sit on juries, the liability to be called as special constables, and the duty to assist the police when called on in order to perform various unpleasant functions.

Frederick Ryland, 'Politics for Girls: Female Suffrage', *The Girl's Own Paper*, 16 May 1896

Lady Dorothy Howard arguing the cause of the suffragettes at a political meeting in 1908

1   Go through the checklist on page 123.

2   Which arguments are biased? Which arguments reveal prejudice?

3   Write a reasoned essay arguing the case either for or against Ryland's point of view.

REACHING A CONCLUSION

In an examination, or in a special study, you will often have to reach a conclusion. This is a summing up of what you know about a topic. A good conclusion will balance different opinions and arguments against each other and then state clearly the verdict of the writer. A good conclusion will also be supported by facts and historical evidence (if this is available). But it will avoid making generalisations based on only one or two examples.

In the extract printed opposite you can read about the visit made by a woman writer to two cotton mills near Bolton in about 1844. These were the only factories she saw but she used them to make this generalisation: 'The factory people are better clothed, better fed, and better conducted than many other classes of working-people.' This conclusion is the exact opposite of the one reached by Lord Ashley (later Earl Shaftesbury) and by other people who tried to improve working conditions in textile mills and coal mines in the early nineteenth century. They knew that some factories were well run, like those of Robert Owen at his mills in New Lanark in Scotland. But the appalling working conditions in many mills, factories, and mines were recorded in writing by hundreds of eyewitnesses. Their evidence reveals:

- dangerous machines left unguarded so that accidents were common
- young children employed to crawl under machines to do dangerous jobs
- women and children doing back-breaking jobs
- employees working very long hours
- tired children making mistakes and causing serious accidents
- children often being beaten when they were tired or when they made mistakes
- air filled with dust so that workers breathed it into their lungs, causing diseases
- a deafening clatter from looms and from other machines
- suffocatingly hot and humid air in summer
- cold and badly-heated factories in winter
- poorly ventilated mines, mills and factories
- gloomy and badly lit workplaces
- dirty buildings often infested with vermin and polluted by waste
- overworked, underfed, and underpaid workers.

The agitation to improve working conditions made some progress with the passing of the Factory Act in 1844. This limited the legal hours of work in textile mills for all women, girls and boys under 18 years. Children under 13 years could only work in a mill on a 'half-time' basis. The Act also demanded that dangerous machines be screened to make them safe to use.

EXERCISES AND ACTIVITIES

Sixteen days after the passing of the Factory Act, *Chambers's Journal* printed this account of a visit to two cotton mills at Turton and Egerton (near Bolton in Lancashire).

> I found the mill a large building, with a wide stone staircase, easy of ascent and very clean. The working rooms are spacious, well-ventilated, and lofty, kept at an equable temperature, and, like all parts of the factory, exceedingly clean. There are a number of windows in each room, indeed so many, that I wondered if they had any window-duty to pay ...
>
> I observed that great care had been bestowed upon the 'boxing-up' of dangerous machinery, and was told that accidents were very rare, and that when they did occur, they were the 'result of the greatest stupidity or negligence'.
>
> After examining everything, I came to the conclusion that the nature of factory labour would have no deteriorating effect on those engaged in it; in which opinion I was confirmed by seeing the healthy appearance of the operatives about me. Many girls who were at work – I may say all, for I saw no exceptions – looked healthy and happy. Their ages, I should think, varied from fourteen to four-and-twenty ...
>
> If an operative has a number of children, he generally endeavours to procure employment for them at the mill where he works, and their united earnings make them very comfortable ...
>
> Now that I have seen the factory people at their work, in their cottages, and in their schools, I am totally at a loss to account for the outcry that has been made against them ...
>
> The millowners, as far as I can judge, are most anxious to contribute to their happiness and welfare, and the operatives themselves seem quite contented with their situation. With respect to infant, or more properly, juvenile labour, I do not see how it can be dispensed with ...
>
> My opinion is, that as long as the masses have to earn their bread by the sweat of their brows, we cannot expect to see them better off, more comfortable, or more happy than the factory operatives of the north of England.
>
> Anonymous woman writer, *Chambers's Journal*,
> 22 June 1844

Inside a cotton textile mill in about 1840

1   Go through the master checklist on page 129.

2   How many cotton mills did she visit? How far apart were they? Did she see a fair selection of mills from all over northern England?

3   What did she base her conclusions on – facts or opinions?

4   What were her conclusions? Make a list of them. Then take each conclusion, point by point, and write a short criticism of it.

5   Which of the list of complaints printed on page 126 does the writer appear to contradict? Do you think she went out of her way to look for 'evidence' which put the employer in a favourable light?

6   After reading this extract there are a number of possible conclusions we might come to. Here are just a few. See if you can add to them.
   ● That conditions were excellent in all cotton textile mills in 1844 (as the writer implies in her article).
   ● That conditions were excellent in some cotton textile mills in 1844.
   ● That the visitor was extremely lucky to visit two rare examples of well-managed textile mills.
   ● That the visitor was hoodwinked by the owners and by the managers in the two mills she visited.
   ● That the visitor was biased and could have had a financial interest in these or other cotton mills.
   ● That the visitor was lying and hoodwinked the editor of the magazine which printed her article.
   Which seems to you to be the most sensible balanced conclusion on the basis of all the facts and evidence provided in the article?

7   Does your conclusion agree with all the facts? If not, why not? Which evidence points to some conclusion other than the one you have reached?

Summary Checklists

Master Checklist — Documentary Evidence

1 What does the source tell you about the past?

2 What is the origin of the source? What type of evidence is it (e.g. diary, letter, newspaper report)? Is it likely to be reliable?

3 Why was the source written? Was it written to justify the writer's actions? Does the writer try to take credit for successes which other people claim for themselves? Does the writer put the blame for failures on to other people?

4 When was the source written? Is it a primary source, dating from the time of the event which it describes? Or is it a secondary source?

5 Is there any clue or statement to show that it is an actual eyewitness account? Was the writer in a good position to say what happened? Does the source agree with other eyewitness accounts of the same event? Are there any reasons for thinking the eyewitness cannot be trusted entirely?

6 If the source was written years after the event, is there any reason to doubt the accuracy of the writer's memory?

7 Which parts of the extract seem to you to be opinions, and not facts which can be proved right or wrong? Are the opinions based on facts or on prejudice? Has the writer used words of approval or disapproval, or colourful or exaggerated phrases, to try to influence the reader?

8 Does the author show any other signs of bias or prejudice? Does the writer appear to take sides in an argument?

9 Are there any obvious mistakes or errors of fact in the extract? Which statements are supported by facts you know about from other sources? Does anything in the extract contradict other sources, or facts which you already know to be true?

10 Does the account give a distorted view of events which actually occurred? Has the author left out facts which tell a different story? Is any part of the extract an obvious lie or exaggeration? Are there any obvious gaps in the evidence, such as missing dates, facts, or personalities?

Checklist — **Pictures from the Past**

1 *Does the picture attempt realistically to portray people, events, buildings, etc., or does it poke fun at them by means of a cartoon or an exaggerated drawing (called a caricature)?*

2 *What does the picture show? What does it tell us about the past?*

3 *When was the picture drawn? Was it drawn at roughly the same time as the event or feature it depicts? Is it a primary source? If no date is given can you estimate roughly the date when it was drawn from the clothes worn by the people in the picture, from styles of vehicles (such as motor cars), or from other clues?*

4 *Why was the picture drawn or painted? Was it simply an illustration (e.g. to accompany a news item or to illustrate a book), is there any reason to think the artist was using the picture to make you feel in a certain way about the events or people depicted? For instance, was it drawn or painted to make you want to protest against an injustice, or to feel excited, or sad, or nostalgic for an old way of life, or patriotic, or self-satisfied, or envious of someone else's way of life?*

5 *Does the picture show something which could not be shown in any other way, such as the interior of a courtroom where photographs are not permitted?*

6 *Even if it looks like a realistic picture, is there any reason to think it is a product of the artist's imagination rather than a portrayal of an actual scene or event?*

7 *If the picture is a cartoon, what was the artist getting at? What does the cartoon tell you about the topic, events or people portrayed? What does it tell you about the attitude of the artist who drew the cartoon or of the magazine which published it?*

Checklist — **Photographs**

1 *What does the photograph show? What does it tell us about the past?*

2 *When and where was the photograph taken? If no date is given, use clues to estimate the date.*

3 *Why was the photograph taken? Is there any reason to think the photographer chose a viewpoint or a subject to make us feel in a certain way about the event or people depicted?*

4   *Is there any sign that the people in the photograph are posing for the photographer? Were they aware of the camera? Does this make any difference to the value of the photograph?*

5   *Is there any reason to think that the photograph is not a typical example of what it appears to show? Is there any reason to think that it may have been altered in any way?*

Checklist — Relics from the Past

1   *What was the purpose of the tool, machine, vehicle, or building you are studying? What was it used for? Why was it built or made?*

2   *Can you date the object or building either exactly or approximately?*

3   *Where is it situated now or where was it found? Where did it come from originally?*

4   *What does it tell us about people in the past?*

Checklist — Maps and Plans

1   *When was the map drawn? What does it show? If it is a special map why was it drawn?*

2   *Is the map accurately drawn? Has it got a scale? If not, work out the scale for yourself. Compare measurements on the old map between three landmarks (e.g. churches) and then compare them with the same measurements on a modern map. In this way you can tell if the map was drawn roughly to scale or not (since the three landmarks will not have moved their position since the date when the old map was drawn).*

3   *What is the particular value of the map (if any) as a source of historical information?*

Checklist — **Statistics**

1   *When and how were the statistics collected? Who collected them? Were they in a position to collect accurate or reliable statistics? Can we be certain they are not guesses, estimates, approximations, or even lies?*

2   *Is it likely that someone else working in exactly the same way would collect the same statistics? If not, why not?*

3   *Are the statistics complete or only a sample of all the possible statistics which could have been recorded?*

4   *Who selected the statistics for use and how were they chosen?*

5   *What do the statistics tell you about the past? What do they prove? If they are quoted to back up a statement, do they really support the conclusions drawn from them by the writer?*

6   *Are the statistics used to support a statement which may be biased or prejudiced?*

7   *If averages are used, do they mean anything? See if you can find out how they were calculated.*

Checklist — **Change**

1   *What was the nature of the change? Was it part of a much bigger change?*

2   *Was it an important and significant change? Did it affect everybody and almost every activity, like the coming of the railway, motor car and telephone? Or did it affect just a section of the community, such as the effect of the means test in the 1930s on the unemployed?*

3   *Who or what benefited from the change? Who or what suffered from the change?*

4   *Did the change take place suddenly, rapidly, steadily, slowly, jerkily, or imperceptibly?*

5   *Did the change affect people mainly because of its social effects, such as on education or health; or mainly because of its economic effects, such as on agriculture or industry; or both?*

Checklist — **Cause and Consequence**

1   *What are the suggested effects and consequences?*

2   *Are these effects and consequences facts which can be proved or disproved? Or are they opinions? For instance, the statement that 'the population of London trebled in size between 1851 and 1931' is a consequence which can be easily proved if you look at the census statistics. But the statement that 'young people were better behaved fifty years ago' is an opinion. It cannot be proved or disproved to everyone's satisfaction.*

3   *What causes of these effects and consequences have been given?*

4   *Which of these causes can be backed up by facts and evidence? Can they be proved or disproved?*

Checklist — **A Reasoned Argument**

1   *List the arguments for.*

2   *List the arguments against.*

3   *Which of these arguments are based on facts and which are opinions? Which can be proved? Which are unprovable?*

4   *Which arguments seem to you to be backed up by the most convincing evidence? Which arguments are weak and unconvincing? Which side has the better case?*

Checklist — **The Link with the Past**

1   *Find out if there are any features, such as buildings, monuments, street names, or house names near your home which link up in some way with the topic.*

2   *Which of your living relatives (if any) were alive for part of the time covered by the topic? What do they remember about this period?*

3   *What things from the past can you find in your local museum or library which link up with this topic?*

Index

CONCEPTS, SKILLS AND SOURCES

accuracy and reliability   23-7
advertisements   7, 27, 65-70
altered evidence   16-19
annals   60
archaeology   47
arguments   123-6

bias   27-35
books, evidence from   7, 12

caricatures   28, 81
cartoons   8, 46, 61, 63, 80, 82, 86,
   87, 91, 111
cause and consequence   117-21
census statistics   74, 100
Checklist
   accuracy and reliability   24
   bias and prejudice   28
   change   110, 132
   cause and consequence   118,
      133
   documentary evidence   53, 129
   evidence from eyewitnesses   41
   facts and opinions   20
   gaps and contradictions   35-6
   historical evidence   9
   links with the past   2, 133
   maps and plans   75, 131
   photographs   94, 130-1
   pictures from the past   81, 130
   reasoned argument   123, 133
   relics from the past   47, 131
   statistics   101, 132
change   16, 108-13
conclusions   126-8
contemporary pictures   78, 80
continuity   109
contradictions   35-9

dating clues   83, 84, 93, 96
diaries   6, 14-15, 17-19, 59-64
differences   104-7
documentary evidence   52-6

election posters   66, 70
ellipsis   17
empathy   114-17
engravings   16, 18, 29, 31, 36, 42,
   44, 72, 78-80, 82, 86-9, 91,
   105, 107, 108, 113, 115, 116,
   120, 121, 128
eyewitnesses   40-6, 92-3

facts   4, 19-23
fiction   71-4
films   97-9
for and against   123-6

gaps   35-9

hearsay evidence   40-6
historical evidence   1, 4-15

imagining the past   114-17
industrial archaeology   47

journals   59-64

law courts   122-3
letters   59-64
links with the past   1-3

maps   74-7
memoirs   64-5
movie films   97-9

newspapers   5, 54-6, 57-9
novels   71-4

opinion polls   100
opinions   19-23
oral history   64-5

paintings   90
photographs (old)   8, 21, 23, 34,
   50, 58, 92-6, 97, 114, 117, 125
pictures   78-91
plans   74-7
posters   52
prejudice   27-35
primary sources   4
proof   19
propaganda   65-70, 97

reasoned argument   123-6
relevance   122-3
reliability   23-7, 40
relics from the past   47-51

sampling   100
secondary sources   4
selection   122-3
similarities   104-7
sound recordings   64, 97
sources   4
spoken history   64-5
statistics   100-3
Summary Checklists, 129-33
summing up, 126-8

video recordings, 98-9

THEMES IN ECONOMIC AND SOCIAL HISTORY

Agriculture
Agricultural Revolution   110-12
farm labourers   41-4
harvesting   95
livestock   102-3
new farming   12-14
village life   92-3

Education
dame schools   7
health in schools   103

Industry
Arkwright, Sir Richard   14-15

coal mining   8, 55-6, 57-9, 100,
   104-7
chemicals   23
domestic woollen industry   120-1
industrial archaeology   47
industrial progress 119-20
textiles   88, 120-1, 126-8

working conditions   90, 104–7,
    126–8

Medicine, Health, and Leisure
cholera   101–2
cleanliness   7, 69
gin drinking   82
health in schools   103
holidays   59
links with past   2–3
street entertainments   94
urban living conditions   114–17

Politics
Chartism   87
elections   70
government   17–19
Irish Troubles   89–90
Peterloo Massacre   45–6

Social Welfare and Reform
cleanliness   7, 69
evictions   89–90
law and order   55, 91
police   91
Poor, the   72–4, 84

town halls   113
unemployment   21–2, 29–32
watchmen   55
workhouse   1, 72–4

Trade and Economy
Bank of England   96

Transport and Communications
airships   93
canals   86
docks   36–9
hansom cabs   49–50
horsebus   96
lifeboats   79
motoring   8, 67, 83
newspapers   5, 57–9
railways   10–12, 33–5
road travel   6
Post Office   52
stage coaches   64
turnpike roads   54–5, 77, 121

Urban Problems
conurbations   112, 121
Georgian towns   71–2, 78, 82
hansom cabs   49–50

housing   48–9, 104–7
living conditions   114–17
overcrowding   82
pollution   23, 88, 117
ribbon development   86
sanitation   61–3, 101–2, 116
street cleaning   51
street lighting   51
urban change   15–16, 74–6, 108–9,
    112

Women and Society
home life   68–9
suffragettes   24–7, 85, 97–9
suffragist movement   124–6

Working-class Movements
Chartists (1848)   87
'Bloody Sunday' (1887)   29–32
Combination Laws (1825)   122–3
General Strike (1926)   57–9
Llanelli (1911)   33–5
London Dock Strike (1889)   36–9
Miners' Strike (1984–5)   55–6
Peterloo Massacre (1819)   45–6